BLACK&DECKER.

Landscape
Design & Construction

CREATIVE
PUBLISHING
international

www.creativepub.com

Contents

Copyright© 1992
Creative Publishing international, Inc.
18705 Lake Drive East
Chanhassen, Minnesota 55317
1-800-328-3895
www.creativepub.com
All rights reserved

Printed in American paper by:
R. R. Donnelley
10

President/CEO: Michael Eleftheriou
Vice President/Publisher: Linda Ball
Vice President/Retail Sales & Marketing:
  Kevin Haas

Managing Editor: Paul Currie
Project Manager: Carol Harvatin
Senior Art Director: Tim Himsel
Art Director: Dave Schelitzche
Editor: Bryan Trandem
Technical Production Editor: Jim Huntley
Copy Editor: Janice Cauley
Contributing Editor: Greg Breining, Mark
  Johanson, Dick Sternberg, John Whitman
Photo Director: Jim Destiche
Shop Supervisor: Phil Juntti
Set Builders: Patrick Kartes, Curtis Lund,
  John Nadeau, Tom Rosch, Mike Shaw,
  Greg Wallace
Director of Development Planning &
  Production: Jim Bindas
Production Manager: Amelia Merz
Production Staff: Adam Esco, Joe Fahey,
  Melissa Grabanski, Eva Hanson, Mike

Hehner, Jeff Hickman, Paul Najlis, Robert
  Powers, Mike Schauer, Nik Wogstad
Studio Manager: Cathleen Shannon
Assistant Studio Manager: Rena Tassone
Lead Photographer: Mark Macemon
Photographers: Rebecca Hawthorne, Rex
  Irmen, John Lauenstein, Mike Parker
Contributing Photographers: Phil Aarrestad,
  Kim Bailey, Paul Herda, Chuck Nields,
  Brad Parker, Susan Roth, Ned Scubic,
  Skyview Photos of America Inc.
Models: Helen Chorolec, Matt Robbey,
  Gary Sandin
Contributing Manufacturers: Anchor Wall
  Systems Inc., Cooper Industries, Lilypons
  Water Gardens, Topnotch Tree Trimmers
Contributing Photography: Anchor Wall
  Systems Inc., Bachman's Landscaping,
  Beuchel Stone Corporation, California

Landscape Construction Projects **48**

NOTICE TO READERS

This book provides useful instructions, but we cannot anticipate all of your working conditions or the characteristics of your materials and tools. For safety, you should use caution, care, and good judgment when following the procedures described in this book. Consider your own skill level and the instructions and safety precautions associated with the various tools and materials shown. Neither the publisher nor Black & Decker® can assume responsibility for any damage to property or injury to persons as a result of misuse of the information provided.

The instructions in this book conform to "The Uniform Plumbing Code," "The National Electrical Code Reference Book," and "The Uniform Building Code" current at the time of its original publication. Consult your local Building Department for information on building permits, codes, and other laws as they apply to your project.

Redwood Assoc., Hickson Corporation (Wolman®), Lilypons Water Gardens, Melroe Company (Bobcat®)

LANDSCAPE DESIGN & CONSTRUCTION
Created by: The editors of Creative Publishing international, Inc., in cooperation with Black & Decker. Black & Decker is a trademark of the Black & Decker Corporation and is used under license.

Books available in this series:
New Everyday Home Repairs, Building Decks, Home Plumbing Projects & Repairs, Basic Wiring & Electrical Repairs, Advanced Home Wiring, Carpentry: Remodeling, Landscape Design & Construction, Built-in Projects for the Home, Refinishing & Finishing Wood, Exterior Home Repairs & Improvements, Home Masonry Repairs & Projects, Building Porches & Patios, Flooring Projects & Techniques, Advanced Deck Building, Advanced Home Plumbing, Remodeling Kitchens, Stonework & Masonry Projects, Finishing Basements & Attics, Sheds, Gazebos & Outbuildings, Complete Guide to Home Wiring, Complete Guide to Home Plumbing, Complete Guide to Building Decks, Complete Guide to Painting & Decorating, Complete Guide to Home Masonry, Complete Guide to Creative Landscapes, Complete Guide to Home Carpentry, Complete Guide to Home Storage, Complete Photo Guide to Home Repair, Complete Photo Guide to Home Improvement, Complete Photo Guide to Outdoor Home Improvement

Library of Congress Cataloging-in-Publication Data

Landscape design & construction.

p. cm.—(Black & Decker home improvement library)
Includes index.
ISBN 0-86573-726-6 (hardcover)
ISBN 0-86573-727-4 (softcover)
1. Landscape architecture.
2. Landscape design.
3. Building—Amateurs' manuals.
4. Landscape gardening.
I. Cy DeCosse Incorporated.
II. Title: Landscape design and construction.
III. Series.
SB473.L355 1992

712—dc20   92-34457

Why Landscape?

Designing and building a successful landscape begins with an understanding of your needs and goals. The purpose can be as simple as improving the appearance of a home by adding a flower garden or as complex as reshaping the entire yard with retaining walls to eliminate erosion. But in any good landscape, the design addresses specific problems and goals.

Like the interior of your home, a well-designed landscape is functional. It should contain different spaces for a variety of activities: eating and entertaining, playing, pursuing hobbies, and relaxing.

When an existing yard does not lend itself well to a variety of uses, the landscape design must solve the problems: add shade to a hot, sunny yard; fix a slope that erodes during every heavy rain shower; build a patio for outdoor cooking and picnicking; create a privacy screen in an exposed backyard.

For many people, landscaping is a means of self-expression. More than any other feature of your home, your yard tells the outside world who you are. The landscape is the first and last thing guests see when visiting your home, and it gives

casual passersby their only view of you and your life-style. A yard with formal garden walls and dense plantings suggests that you are a private person, while a wide walkway leading across an open lawn welcomes visitors to your home.

Designing and building your own landscape can be time-consuming, but it doesn't require expert skills. For this reason, most homeowners can do the work themselves and enjoy a big payback on their

investment. In fact, one recent survey by the American Association of Nurserymen claims that investing $5000 in plants and landscape materials can add up to $30,000 to the value of a $100,000 home. Real estate professionals believe that new landscaping is the single most important improvement a homeowner can make. You'll also find that do-it-yourself landscaping is a lot of fun.

Quality of landscaping dramatically affects the appeal of similar houses. The homes shown here are located only a short distance apart, but one is not yet landscaped (right), while the other has a simple, well-designed landscape that is beginning to mature (above). In the unlandscaped home, the sharp lines of the house abruptly meet the lawn, making the home seem stark and out of place. The other home has shrubs and planting areas to soften the transition between house and yard and make the home seem more inviting.

Finish a New Yard

Newly built home usually comes with a finished lawn, but little additional landscaping.

Starting from scratch with a bare, empty lot is a challenge for a home landscaper, but it also offers the best opportunity to be creative. Because there are few existing features to work around, you will find it easier to build a yard that reflects the interests of your family and meets the demands of your life-style.

Economical landscape begins modestly but has plenty of room for adding features as your interests, budget, and landscaping skills grow. Shade trees are small, fast-growing birches and maples. Inexpensive split-rail fence and planting area set the yard boundaries. Interlocking block retaining walls create terraces that someday may hold a flower garden. Beds of crushed stone planted with shrubs help the house and lawn blend together.

Low-maintenance landscape is designed for the homeowner with little time for yard work. This landscape features a large wrap-around patio made with brick pavers set in sand. Timber retaining walls help manage problem slopes in the backyard. Large planting areas bounded with plastic edging reduce mowing chores, and are covered with landscape fabric and crushed rock to prevent weed growth. Hardy shrubs and shade-tolerant impatiens were chosen because they require little care.

Showcase landscape (left) requires a large investment of time and money initially, but provides a finished look right away. This landscape features a large patio and walkways made from brick pavers, retaining walls made from boulders, and garden steps made from timbers and bricks.

Too much direct sun can make your deck or patio uncomfortably hot in the summer months.

Control Sunlight & Wind

Establishing comfortable levels of sunlight and wind is essential to a successful landscape. Grass and flowering plants thrive under moderate sunlight, but few plants can survive constant, direct sun. Gentle breezes help cool a yard, but harsh winds can make outdoor living nearly impossible.

Control sunlight and wind by using arbors, trellises, and fences in your landscape design, and by positioning large shrubs and trees in strategic locations.

Fences made from interrupted panels (right) or staggered boards (page 101) can break strong winds into cooling breezes. A solid fence is less effective as a windbreak, because the winds simply blow up and over the fence.

Arbors (left) covered with wood strips or lattice panels diffuse bright sunlight into a dappled mixture of light and shadow. Vines planted on an arbor provide deep shade. An arbor works well as a sunscreen over a deck, patio, or children's play area.

Trellises block wind and provide shade for outdoor living areas. For dappled shade, build a trellis from lattice panels; for dense shade, plant climbing vines along the base of the trellis.

Lack of privacy is a common landscape-related complaint of homeowners in cities and suburbs.

Provide Privacy

Privacy structures like fences, trellises, and garden walls dramatically change the look and function of a landscape. Even in the noisiest of urban neighborhoods, a sturdy fence trained with climbing vines can provide a quiet, personal retreat.

Versatile landscapes include both private spaces and open, social areas, but your choice of privacy structures depends on your life-style. For an attractive, visual boundary that does not impede your view, you can build a low rubble-stone wall. For complete privacy, build a 6-ft.-high solid fence around your entire yard.

Fences built with 6-ft.-tall panels are the best choice for creating total privacy and improving home security. A solid fence fronted by shrubs or planted with climbing vines also makes a good sound barrier.

Trellises (left) together with trees and shrubs provide an inexpensive, attractive privacy screen around selected areas of your landscape, such as a deck, patio, or children's play area. For even more privacy, plant climbing vines on your trellis.

Garden walls are an attractive alternative to fences. Low garden walls form boundaries without blocking your view. In large yards, garden walls can help define different living areas.

Mowing grass is difficult and dangerous on a steeply sloped lawn.

Manage a Sloped Yard

Gentle slopes make a landscape more interesting, but steep hills create problems requiring special landscape solutions. Yards with sharp slopes seem small because they have less flat, usable space. And because hillsides make it difficult to plant and maintain grass, shrubs, or flowers, the soil erodes easily.

Retaining walls, terraces, and garden steps help you turn a problem hillside into an interesting and attractive landscape feature.

Retaining walls increase the amount of flat, usable yard space, while helping to control erosion. In addition, the attractive stone and wood products used in retaining walls add color, shape, pattern, and texture to your yard.

Garden steps and paths (left) make it easier and safer to walk between different areas of a sloped yard. By improving access to all parts of the yard, steps and paths can make your landscape seem larger. Steps and paths direct the eye as well as the feet, giving a sense of unity and organization to a landscape.

Terraces made of two or more retaining walls are a good solution for high slopes. The flat terraces provide space for planting flowers, shrubs, or lawn grass.

Create New Living Space

Outdoor living is difficult if your landscape does not provide spaces for the activities you enjoy.

With creative landscaping, you can make versatile outdoor "rooms" perfect for cooking, eating, playing, or just reading and relaxing.

A landscape design can be planned around a single favorite pastime, like gardening or outdoor sports, but most good landscapes are designed to support a variety of activities.

Walkways, paths, and steps form outdoor hallways that connect the house with heavily used areas of the yard, helping to unify a landscape design.

Attached patios (left) make your house seem larger, and are ideal for outdoor entertaining and dining.

Detached patios create private outdoor dens for quiet relaxation. A detached patio can be connected to other areas of the yard with a walkway.

Garden area

Play area

Dining & socializing

Make an outdoor "floor plan" when designing your landscape. Think of each area of your yard as an outdoor room, and plan your landscape so it includes spaces for favorite activities. The front yard, like a formal living room, often is a decorative space used to welcome guests to your home, but the backyard usually serves as private recreational space for family and friends.

Landscape Design & Planning

Planning your own landscape is easy once you understand that landscaping is really nothing more than "remodeling" a yard. Design your landscape using the same common-sense techniques you use when remodeling or decorating the interior of your home.

Like the blueprint for a well-planned house, a good landscape has clearly defined areas for different activities. For a family that enjoys cooking and eating outdoors, a patio serves as a second kitchen and dining room. If you like to read the newspaper outdoors on sunny mornings, include an outdoor "study" with garden furniture. An outdoor "recreation room" can be a flat section of lawn large enough for a volleyball net. Your outdoor "living room" might be a carefully maintained section of lawn bounded by flower gardens and shade trees.

Outdoor spaces can be carpeted with grass, ground cover, or flowers. They can have "ceilings" made from overhanging trees or wood

arbors. Fences, trellises, garden walls, or large planting beds can form walls between different spaces. Visualize the traffic patterns between areas, and plan outdoor "hallways" (sidewalks, paths, and garden stairs) between heavily used spaces.

Good landscapes are a combination of function and beauty. Decorate your outdoor landscape just as you do the interior of your home—by furnishing it with materials, colors, and textures that blend together and create a feeling of unity and visual interest.

Consider each of the following elements when designing your landscape:

- Function (pages 18 to 21)
- Composition (pages 22 to 23)
- Style (pages 24 to 25)
- Structures (pages 26 to 27)
- Materials (pages 28 to 31)
- Plant choices (pages 32 to 35)

Ornate landscape appeals to the enthusiastic home gardener who enjoys working outdoors. The yard is meant to be seen and enjoyed by neighbors and passersby, so the property contains no fences. A large planting island with formally arranged flowers serves as a focal point for the landscape. The trees are ornamental specimens that provide bright seasonal color. Brick-paver walkways lead through beds of ground cover and perennial flowers to connect the three main outdoor living areas: **1.** A brick-paver patio bounded by a cut-stone retaining walls and garden steps. **2.** A decorative landscape pond with a stone bench. **3.** A small detached patio sheltered by an overhead arbor.

Landscape Design
Function

When designing your yard, consider the *function* of your landscape—how well it satisfies your interests and needs. A landscape, no matter how attractive, cannot be considered successful unless the yard is useful for the way you live.

Landscaping tastes are very personal, so consider your life-style carefully as you design your yard. Do you enjoy gardening and yard work, or do you regard it as an annoying chore you would rather avoid? Do you like to entertain outdoors, or do you prefer quiet, intimate spaces?

Does bright sunlight on an open lawn appeal to you, or are you more attracted to a shady glade of ferns? The photos and drawings on the following pages show how one yard can be designed in a variety of ways to match different life-styles.

In some yard designs, a single function provides the organizing theme for the landscape. For example, an avid gardener might design a yard devoted exclusively to planting areas. Most good landscapes, however, have more flexible designs. By providing spaces for a variety of activities, a landscape can appeal to the varying tastes of different family members. With careful planning, even the smallest of yards can serve many interests.

Privacy landscape provides a quiet retreat from the outside world. A tall fence and perimeter shrubs shelter the yard from outside sights and sounds. A loose-material path provides a casual link between living areas.

This yard has three clearly defined living areas: **1.** A large patio, sheltered with an overhead arbor and bordered by landscape contours used as planting areas. **2.** An open, sunny area ideal for private sunbathing or outdoor sports. **3.** A quiet, isolated flower garden with a garden seat, screened from the rest of the yard by a trellis.

Family-use landscape is structured for an active, growing household with a variety of interests. A low picket fence helps confine small children and family pets without restricting the expansive look of the yard. A large specimen tree (page 35) creates a focal point and balances the landscape.

This yard has five distinct living areas: **1.** A large patio with overhead arbor to provide space for eating and socializing. **2.** A children's play area with a timber sandbox and an arbor to give shade. **3.** An expansive open lawn area for outdoor sports. **4.** A sunny garden area with a storage shed and raised planting areas. **5.** A terraced flower garden with garden steps and pathway leading to a gate.

Food-grower's landscape is attractive as well as practical. Instead of a fence, a hedge of raspberry bushes borders the back edge of the yard. The compost container is covered with lattice panels for a more attractive appearance.

This yard has five growing areas: **1.** An orchard area with fruit trees that provide shade and seasonal color as well as food. **2.** A patio with containers and border beds for aromatic, flowering herbs. **3.** A sunny garden area with raised planting beds for vegetables. **4.** A trellis-and-arbor used to hold climbing fruits and vegetables, like grapes or peas. **5.** Landscape contours used for low, creeping vines, like cucumbers or squash.

Party-giver's landscape has spaces for a variety of social gatherings. It includes large trees that offer cooling shade for daylight gatherings, and a system of low-voltage light fixtures that let you enjoy nighttime activities.

This yard has three areas devoted to social activities, connected to each other by walkways and garden steps: **1.** An intimate upper patio area with a whirlpool spa. **2.** A larger lower patio for groups of people. **3.** A detached patio surrounded by garden walls, used as a quiet retreat from the rest of the yard.

Country meadow
landscape uses natural materials for a unified, rustic look. Low rubble-stone walls form a natural-looking border, and a landscape contour breaks up the flatness of the yard.

This yard has four defined areas: **1.** A flagstone patio, bordered with a low stone retaining wall. **2.** An expansive, open lawn area with irregular, curved border designed to resemble a rural grazing meadow. **3.** Groups of birch trees and evergreens that create a realistic wooded area. **4.** A large planting area containing perennial flowers and wildflowers arranged in irregular groups for a natural look.

Low-maintenance landscape satisfies the needs of a busy homeowner who has little time for yard work. The fence is made from natural cedar split-rails that need no paint or stain. An underground sprinkler system waters plants automatically. Sloped areas are managed with a short retaining wall made from durable interlocking block.

This yard has three well-defined areas: **1.** A patio made from cast concrete pavers that require little upkeep. **2.** A small, easy-to-mow lawn area with plastic edging. **3.** Large planting areas, covered with landscape fabric and crushed rock to inhibit weeds, and planted with hardy, easy-to-maintain shrubs and perennial flowers.

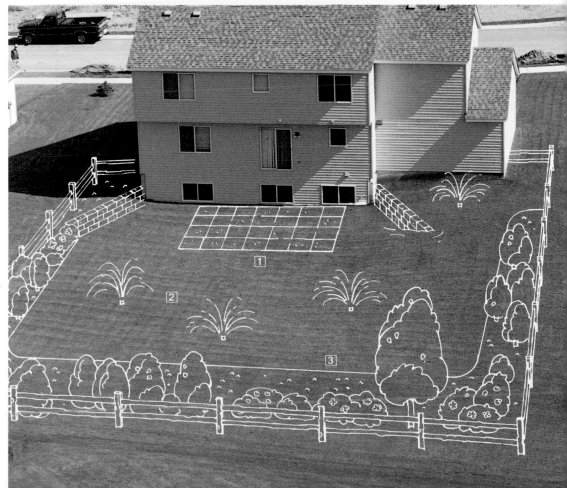

Think about scale. Scale refers to the relative size of objects in a landscape. In the landscape shown here, the owner has arranged the plantings so the larger lilacs and tall bushes are near the back, with smaller shrubs and flowers in front.

Create focal points. Use contrasting colors and distinctive accents to draw visual attention to a few areas of your yard. A trellis-and-arbor and a flower-bed island with birdbath serve as focal points in this landscape.

Repeat yourself. Good landscapes echo similar shapes, colors, and textures to give a feeling of unity. In this landscape, repeating elements include shrubs pruned to distinctive shapes, rows of identical flowers, and a continuous edging made of cast concrete pavers.

Landscape Design

Composition

Landscape designers and architects know that people enjoy landscapes in which the elements are arranged (composed) in familiar, easily recognized patterns. These patterns of composition—including contrast, repetition, and balance—are similar to the principles used by artists and interior designers.

Landscape professionals stress the value of balance in a landscape. Try to plan your yard so it balances elements that are roughly equal in size and shape, but avoid perfectly symmetrical arrangements that look unnatural.

Landscape design is a personal choice, not an exact science, so plan the composition of your yard according to your own tastes—not those of a designer who may never even see your yard.

If you have friends or neighbors with landscaped yards you admire, spend some time studying these sites and try to pinpoint the elements that you find attractive. The information shown on these pages may help you understand why some landscapes are more appealing than others.

Keep it simple. Landscapes with a limited number of plants and structures arranged in groups are easier to view and appreciate than those cluttered with dozens of different types of plants and materials. The simple, attractive landscape shown here is easy to build and requires little maintenance.

Create contrast. Add visual interest to a landscape by careful use of contrasting textures, shapes, sizes, and colors. In general, design your landscape so large or coarse-textured items stand behind smaller items or those with more subtle textures. Use contrast selectively: a landscape with too many contrasting elements looks random and unplanned.

Use curves. Balance the long, straight lines found in most houses by designing your landscape with curved edges for gardens, lawns and walkways.

Control color. Choose plants and materials with colors that harmonize and balance each other. In the yard shown above, the greens of the lawn and shrubs are balanced with a long row of pink annual begonias that draw the eye from the back of the landscape into a dramatic bed of impatiens.

Landscape Design
Style

The home itself is the largest element of any yard, so keep the house style in mind when planning your landscape. Pay particular attention to the size and shape of landscape elements relative to the house, and choose materials that

A: Rural, cottage-style home is well suited to natural landscape materials and an informal style that includes many trees and shrubs. In this home, the low picket fence, arbor, and deck are built with unfinished wood that matches the rustic style of the wood-shingle siding. The brick pavers used for the patio and walkways complement the earth-tones that dominate the landscape.

B: English-Tudor home has irregular shapes and lines that look best with a balanced, unified landscape. In this yard, the circular arrangement of the retaining walls, lawn, and shrubs helps balance the sharp angles of the house. The stone used in the front retaining walls resembles the masonry found on the house. To copy the wooded look of the surrounding neighborhood, this yard includes many trees and a rustic boulder retaining wall.

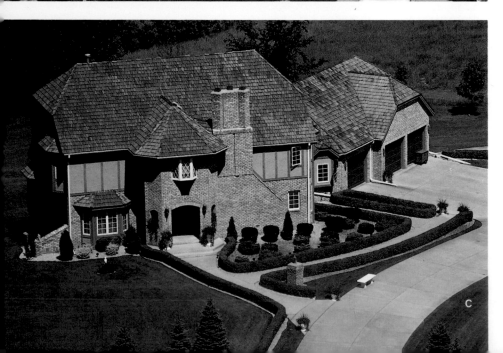

C: French country estate home style calls for a very formal, strictly balanced landscape. In this landscape, the circular drive, formal entry walk, carefully pruned hedges, ornamental shrub garden, and the paired groups of potted plants all contribute to the aristocratic look of the property.

complement the building materials visible on your house.

Also consider the surrounding setting when designing your own yard. If your neighborhood has an attractive, consistent landscape style, you can make your own yard look bigger and more natural by following this style.

These six photos show examples of how home styles and neighborhood setting can influence landscape design.

D: Ranch-style home features retaining-wall terraces that echo the low, horizontal structure of the house. The absence of sidewalks and walkways and the use of landscape timbers make this yard seem like a natural extension of the surrounding rural landscape. For the loose-fill material in the planting areas, the owners chose gray gravel that matches the colors of the roof and siding.

E: Chateau-style home requires bold landscaping to match the sheer size of the house. In this yard, the fortresslike retaining wall helps balance the massive house and garage, and is shaped to echo the curved lines of the walkway. The loose-fill bark used in the planting area matches the color of the roofing material. To avoid clashing with the vivid patterns and colors on the house, the plants were chosen for their simple shapes and colors.

F: Sprawling farmhouse style of this home requires expansive landscaping with wide-open views. The landscape materials used here (wood pickets for the rear fence and small boulders for the front retaining wall) match the traditional materials used in large farmsteads. To soften the transition between the house and lawn, shrubs and small trees are planted in loose-fill gravel beds that match the color of the siding.

Structures

Walls, fences, pathways, and other structures made of wood and stone form the framework for many landscapes. In contrast to the seasonal changes of plants, landscape structures provide a feeling of permanence and help anchor the overall design.

In addition, wood and stone add interesting new colors, textures, and patterns to your landscape. Choosing the right materials for your landscape structures is crucial to good landscape design. See pages 28 to 31 for more information on common landscape construction materials.

Retaining walls are used primarily to solve problems relating to slope—for example, to eliminate troublesome mowing chores or prevent erosion. But retaining walls also add visual interest to a yard. On flat yards, you can make dramatic raised planting areas using retaining wall materials like interlocking block, natural stone, or landscape timbers.

Common Landscape Structures

Fences and free-standing walls define landscape boundaries, create privacy, and block sun and wind. A fence surrounding the entire yard helps unify the landscape. See pages 66 to 71 and 100 to 109.

Trellises and arbors create shady, private areas in a landscape. Usually made from lattice panels or wood strips, trellises and arbors add interesting geometric patterns to a yard, and often are used as a framework for climbing plants. See pages 110 to 113.

Walkways and paths are used to direct traffic between different areas in a yard. Because they lead the eye as well as the feet, walkways give a feeling of visual unity to a landscape. See pages 74 to 81.

Garden steps can be attractive as well as functional. Steps help link different living areas in a split-level landscape, and their strong horizontal lines draw visual attention. See pages 82 to 89.

Patios provide living space for cooking, eating, and entertaining. An attached patio with sweeping curves helps soften the hard, straight lines that dominate most houses. See pages 90 to 99.

Garden ponds catch the eye and create a feeling of tranquility. They also provide a setting for unusual plants and can be used to attract wildlife. See pages 114 to 121.

Interlocking block (below) is made from molded concrete that is split to provide a rough face resembling natural stone. Available in several colors and sizes, interlocking block is used for both straight and curved retaining walls, terraces, and raised planting beds. Interlocking-block walls create bold geometric patterns.

Concrete block is available in plain or decorative types. This durable building material is used often for free-standing garden walls. The hard, plain look of a concrete block wall can be softened with climbing plants or a surface application of stucco or stone veneer.

Poured concrete is durable and less expensive than other paving products. Although concrete is plain in appearance, it is easy to maintain, making it a popular choice for walkways, patios, walls, and steps.

Landscape Design
Materials

Stone, masonry, and wood are primary building materials for landscape construction. Stone and masonry give your landscape structures a feeling of permanence. Wood has a natural, warm look, is easy to shape, and can be painted or stained to match existing structures.

Whenever possible, choose landscape materials that either match or complement the materials already used on your home. For example, if you have a brick home, a patio made from similar brick will be more appealing than a poured concrete slab. Or, if you have a Tudor-style house

with exposed beams, a retaining wall built from rough timbers is more appropriate than a wall built from interlocking concrete blocks.

Man-made stone products cast from concrete are a good choice for landscape structures, considering the increasing price and dwindling supplies of forest timber and natural stone. Interlocking concrete block, brick pavers, and other manufactured stone products are widely available, easy to install, and very durable.

If you prefer the look of natural stone, try to select a type of rock that is common in your geographic region. Local stone makes your landscape look natural, and it is much less expensive than stone that must be shipped long distances.

Interlocking pavers made from molded concrete are used in patios, walkways, and driveways. Available in a variety of colors and shapes, interlocking pavers are a good way to add distinctive patterns to a landscape.

Brick is an elegant, traditional building material made from molded, oven-dried clay. Available in many styles, brick is used to build patios, walkways, edging, and free-standing garden walls.

Terra cotta and adobe are molded clay products that are dried in the sun. They are used for patios, walkways, and garden walls. These products have a porous surface that can be damaged by water, so terra cotta and adobe are best suited for very dry climates.

Concrete pavers are made from poured concrete, and are available in many decorative shapes, textures, and colors. Inexpensive and easy to install, concrete pavers are used for patios, walkways, and steps.

Crushed
gravel

Smooth
river
gravel

Cut stone
(granite)

Flagstone

Glacial
rubble stone

Accent rock
(quartz blend)

Natural Stone

Gravel comes in
two forms: rough gravel
made by crushing larger
rocks, and smooth gravel
usually dredged from rivers.
Gravel is sorted by size, and has
many landscape uses. Applied as a
loose layer, gravel makes an informal, easy-
to-maintain pathway. Laid in large beds,
gravel lends a relaxed feeling to a landscape while providing texture and color.

Cut stone, sometimes call ashlar, is natural
stone that has been cut into cubic shapes.
Marble, hard limestone, and granite (shown
here) are popular for cut stone. Cut stone is used
for both mortared or unmortared walls, patios or
walkways. It is an expensive, top-quality building
material that gives landscape structures an
elegant, timeless appearance.

Flagstone is uncut sedimentary stone that has natu-
ally flat surfaces. Limestone, slate, and shale are common types of flagstone. Flagstone works well with
large, expansive landscapes, and is used for walkways, patios, and steps. It is a durable, but expensive,
paving material.

Rubble stone is any type of irregular, uncut
rock collected from fields, gullies, or stream
beds. It can include boulders, glacial debris,
rough pieces of quartz or granite, random
pieces of limestone or sandstone, or
even volcanic rock. Rubble stone often
is used in garden walls and retaining walls, and works best in informal, rustic landscapes. Rubble
stone is cheaper than cut stone.

Accent rock is distinctive
natural stone used as decoration rather than as a building
material. Large, colorful rocks
can be partially buried in a
planting area or lawn to add
visual interest. Accent
rocks can range in size
from small 20-lb.
pieces to enormous
boulders weighing
more than a ton.

Wood

Wood and bark chips are used for loose-fill on soft pathways or as a ground cover for planting areas. Wood and bark chips are inexpensive and lend a relaxed, casual look to a landscape.

Pressure-treated pine contains pesticides and wood preservatives to make it last. Less expensive than cedar and redwood, pressure-treated pine is used to build fences, retaining walls, raised planting beds, and garden steps. Most pressure-treated pine is green when new, but gradually weathers to a neutral gray. Or, it can be stained to resemble redwood or cedar. In some areas, treated pine also is available in a dark-brown color.

Cedar is a soft wood with a rough texture. It has natural resistance to decay and insect damage, and is used for fences, trellises, and arbors. Use cedar in above-ground structures only: where wood will be in contact with the ground, use pressure-treated lumber instead.

Redwood is a smooth-grained wood with a natural resistance to insects and decay. It is used for above-ground structures, like fences, trellises, and overhead arbors. Avoid using redwood where a structure will be in contact with the ground: for these applications, use pressure-treated wood instead. Because of high demand and dwindling supplies, redwood is becoming more expensive.

Redwood bark chips

Pressure-treated pine

Wood chips

Cedar

Redwood

Choose plants suited for your climate and yard. Nursery plants carry identification tags describing the plant and its sun and soil requirements. When ordering plants from mail-order suppliers, refer to a geographic zone map for information on plant hardiness. All zone maps are based on U.S. Department of Agriculture statistics, but the map information varies from supplier to supplier. When ordering, always refer to the zone map in the supplier's catalog, and check with a local nursery to make sure the plant is hardy in your area.

Plant Selection

Plants provide the final decoration for your landscape. By virtue of their yearly growth and seasonal color, plants provide an element of change in a yard.

Beginning landscapers often make the mistake of using too many different plant species in their designs. As you do with any landscape design element, strive for simplicity when choosing plants. Remember that plants grow: find out each plant's mature size and leave enough room around plantings so the landscape does not smother itself within a few years.

The following pages show the basic categories of plants used in landscaping, but remember there are many dozens of different species in each category. Each plant species has different environmental needs, so consider your climate, soil composition, and sun exposure when choosing trees, shrubs, and flowers for your landscape. Visit a large local nursery or arboretum, or talk with members of a local gardening club, to find out which plants are best suited to your conditions.

Avoid exotic plant species not commonly found in your area. Some exotic species, especially unusual aquatic plants purchased through mail order, can spread into the wild, threatening native plants and animals.

Arrange plants in groups (photo, left). A yard that features shrubs, flowers, and trees placed in a few well-balanced groups is easy to appreciate at a glance. Use a hose or rope and potted plants to lay out planting areas.

Basic Plant Types

Grass lawns are used in most landscape designs. A carpet of grass provides a pleasant, versatile surface for outdoor activities, and adds a unifying color and texture to a landscape. Lawns look best when bordered with informal groups of trees or perennial flowers that create a natural, meadowlike appearance. All grass species require at least some direct sunlight to thrive.

Ground covers provide an attractive covering for areas where grass does not grow, like steep hillsides or heavily shaded areas. Common types of ground cover include spurge (shown above), ferns, hostas, and periwinkle. Ground covers should be used in low-traffic areas only. They take several years to become fully established, but require little maintenance.

Broadleaf trees, like the locust shown above, are large, dominant features of a landscape. Deciduous broadleaf trees provide bright autumn color before losing their leaves for the winter. Make sure to choose species that will be in scale with your house when they mature. Seedlings require 15 to 25 years to mature, so you may want to buy well-established trees and have them planted by professionals. Trees block sunlight, so consider how the shady areas around trees will affect other plants.

Needle evergreen trees (conifers) add strong, geometric shapes to a landscape. Common evergreens include the spruces (shown above), pines, and firs. In cold climates, evergreens provide much-needed winter color. The height of mature trees ranges from 6 ft. to more than 150 ft. Evergreen needles are strongly acidic, so growing grass or flowers directly under evergreen trees is difficult.

(continued next page)

Shrubs and bushes are medium-size woody plants that bridge the visual gap between large structures or trees and low-lying flowers or lawns. Planted individually or in groups, shrubs provide color and shape, and require little care. Planted in rows, shrubs can be pruned to create a formal privacy hedge. Deciduous shrubs, such as potentilla and spirea, lose their leaves in the autumn, while evergreens, such as arborvitae and juniper, provide color year-round.

Aquatic plants thrive in and around artificial garden ponds. Some plants, including water lilies (shown above), do well in water several feet deep, while other species, such as water iris and water poppy, thrive in shallow water or boggy soil.

Climbing vines often are trained to grow up trellises and arbors, providing an effective, attractive screen. They also are used to soften the look of fences and walls. Although they take several growing seasons to become established, vines require little maintenance. Common vines include clematis (shown above), Boston ivy, wisteria, and wild grape.

Succulent plants have fleshy tissues that store moisture, making them well-suited for arid climates. Noted for their exotic shapes and colors, succulents range in size from low, ground-cover plants, like hens and chicks (shown above), to the huge saguaro cactus that can grow to 60 ft. Some succulents will survive in cooler climates, where they commonly are used in rock gardens.

Herbs and vegetables usually are planted to provide food, but they also add attractive textures and fragrances to your yard. Many herbs, like garlic chives (shown above), also have attractive flowers. Even small urban landscapes can include vegetables and herbs grown in containers.

Specimen plants include any decorative or unusual species of tree, shrub, or flower used to draw attention in a yard. Specimen plants can include cacti and other succulents (shown above); flowering trees, like magnolias and flowering crabs; flowering bushes, like azaleas and rhododendrons; and climbing roses. For best impact, limit the number of specimen plants you use, and design your landscape so they are easily seen.

Perennials grow and spread from the same roots each year, making them a good choice for low-maintenance landscapes. Most perennials, like phlox, daisies, and sedum (all shown above), provide subtle color throughout the growing season. Bulb or tuber types, such as iris, tulip, and gladiolus, provide vivid color in the spring and early summer. Perennial flowers look best in border beds and informal groups.

Annual flowers must be planted anew each year, but they grow much faster than perennials. Available in hundreds of species, annuals provide bright color throughout the year. These versatile plants are well suited for informal flower beds, formal garden arrangements, and for planting in hanging baskets and other containers.

Plan ahead and be patient when designing your new landscape. Remember that plants grow and spread, and stone and wood structures change appearance as they weather. Landscape designers say that it takes at least five years for a landscape to reach its finished look. In the landscape shown above (inset), the owner chose to plant a few well-spaced shrubs and perennials. Several years later (larger photo), this attractive yard is approaching maturity without being overcrowded.

Landscape Planning

Once you have reviewed the basic landscape design ideas on pages 17 to 35, you are ready to plan your own yard. A detailed landscape plan takes time to develop, but helps ensure smooth work and successful results. Your finished plans should include detailed drawings, an accurate budget, a list of materials, and a realistic time schedule.

Evaluate your existing landscape carefully as you begin to plan. To save money and time, plan the new landscape so it makes use of existing features that are both attractive and functional—a favorite flower garden, a garden walk, or a healthy tree, for example. You can transplant many hardy bushes and most perennial flowers

from one part of your yard to another to fit a new landscape plan.

Although most of the projects shown in this book can be done without a work permit, always check with the local inspections office before you begin. If a building permit is required, you will need to have the inspector check your work.

Follow these steps when creating your landscape plan:

• Testing landscape ideas (pages 38 to 39)
• Drawing a plan (pages 40 to 41)
• Budgeting your time and money (pages 42 to 43)
• Acquiring tools and materials (pages 44 to 47)

Tips for Landscape Planning

Obey local "setback" regulations when planning fences, walls, and other landscape structures. The setback distance, determined by the local Building Code, prevents you from building any structure too close to property lines. Call your community inspections office to learn about any other restrictions on how and where you can build landscape structures.

Talk to your neighbors about your landscaping plans. Many projects, like building a fence, or planting a large shade tree or hedge, will affect neighbors as well as yourself. Keep the peace and avoid legal disputes by making sure your neighbors do not object to your plans.

Locate buried utility lines. Public utilities, like power, telephone, gas, and water companies, are required by law to inspect your site on request and mark locations of all buried lines. If your project requires digging or excavation, make sure your work will not interfere with underground utility lines.

Measure your yard, including the locations of all permanent landscape features. Accurate yard measurements are essential for drawing plans and estimating the quantities and costs of materials.

Testing Landscape Ideas

Making simple sketches is the traditional method for testing landscape ideas, but you will get a better idea of how your landscape will look if you also go outdoors and model your plans in the yard itself. For example, you can use stakes and sheets of cardboard to illustrate how a fence, trellis, or free-standing wall will look.

While testing your ideas, look at your landscape from many different angles. View the yard from downstairs and upstairs windows, from the front side-walk and the street, and from neighboring yards. Consider how time-of-day and seasonal changes will affect shade patterns in the yard.

Use a garden hose to test the layout of walkways, patios, planting beds, ponds, and other landscape features. When planning a curved walkway (above), use pieces of wood lath cut to the same length to maintain an even width.

Buy or borrow sample materials, like interlocking blocks or brick pavers, and arrange them on-site to see which materials complement the existing materials in your yard and house.

Tips for Testing Landscape Ideas

Make simple sketches by enlarging a photograph of your yard on a photocopier, then copying the outline onto tracing paper. Next, find magazine or catalog photos of plants and landscape structures, and trace them onto the drawing to see how they might look in your yard. If necessary, use a photocopier to shrink or enlarge the photos to the proper scale before tracing them.

Use brown wrapping paper to model patios, walkways, and other paved surfaces on your yard. You can test different paver patterns by tracing the designs on the paper with colored chalk.

Test layouts for planting areas using potted plants and shrubs. This also can help you determine which plant species look best in your yard.

Landscape Planning
Drawing a Plan

Accurate and detailed drawings of your landscape plan help you organize your work and make it easier to estimate quantities and costs of materials. If your project needs a building permit, the inspector who issues the permit will ask to see your drawn plans.

If you do not know the exact locations of property lines, prevent possible legal disputes by having your property surveyed.

If you are planning a large project that will be completed in stages, draw a separate plan for each stage of the project. These drawings are especially helpful if you consult a landscape designer. Many nurseries have designers on staff who review plans and offer free advice to customers.

Use an original blueprint, if you have one, and copy the outline of your house and yard onto tracing paper. If you do not have a blueprint, use drafting paper (inset), available at art supply stores, to draw a scaled plan.

Landscape Plan Symbols

Ground cover	Lawn grass	Annual flowers	Perennial flowers	Deciduous trees, shrubs	Evergreen trees, shrubs
Vegetables	Hedge	Vines	Timbers		
Interlocking block	Cut stone	Flagstone	Concrete block	Boulders	Brick pavers
Concrete pavers	Wood decking	Wood chips	Gravel	Water	Bench
Fence	Wire / Chain-link	Gate	Trellis	Arbor	Steps

Use landscape symbols, shown above, to indicate the location of structures and plants on your plan drawing. These standard symbols are used by landscape professionals and building inspectors.

How to Draw a Plan

1 Draw an outline of your property to scale on drafting paper, or trace the outline from an original blueprint. Make sure the property lines are accurate (consult a surveyor, if necessary). Mark all underground and overhead utility lines on the plan.

2 Add the buildings, driveways, sidewalks, and other main features of your property to the plan. Include accurate measurements of the features.

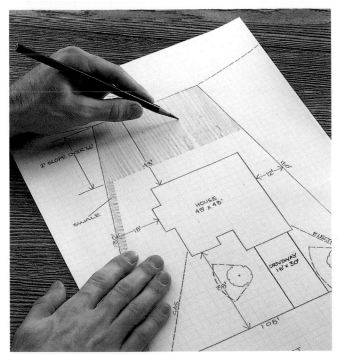

3 Show any existing yard features that will be retained in the new landscape. Mark low spots, hills, and contours with pencil shading, and show the shade patterns of trees and buildings. Compass directions on the plan will be helpful if you choose to consult a designer.

4 Add all the proposed structures and plants. Make a list of all the materials you will need.

Save time by hiring a professional to do difficult, time-consuming chores, or to haul large amounts of gravel, sand, or topsoil. Professionals have special equipment to do these jobs quickly.

Budgeting Your Time & Money

For large landscaping projects, you may want to spread out the expense and time by dividing the project into smaller jobs that can be completed over a period of months or even years. If you choose to work this way, make sure you begin with a good overall landscaping plan. First do the large projects, like retaining walls, then move to the smaller structures and planting projects.

Make accurate estimates of the materials you need, because leftover materials like concrete, brick, and stone usually cannot be returned to suppliers. To save money, try to coordinate your landscape projects with those of neighbors so you can take advantage of volume discounts on brick, stone, sod, and other materials.

Tips for Saving Money

Collect free materials. For example, you can get wood chips, suitable for mulching planting areas or covering pathways, from tree trimmers, power companies, and other utility companies. Farmers or housing developers may let you collect rubble stone. Paving brick may be salvaged from demolition sites. Neighbors who are avid gardeners sometimes have extra flower bulbs and other perennials. If you are removing old landscape structures, consider reusing the materials.

Save money by hauling materials yourself with a pick-up truck or trailer. Shipping charges for small volumes of gravel, sand, or topsoil can be more expensive than the materials themselves.

Estimating & Ordering Materials

Use this chart to help you estimate the materials you will need for landscaping projects. Sizes and weights of materials may vary, so consult your supplier for more detailed information on estimating materials.

If you are unfamiliar with the gravel and stone products available in your area, visit a sand-and-gravel supplier to see the products first-hand.

When sand, gravel, and other bulk materials are delivered, place them on a tarp to protect your yard. Make sure the tarp is as close to the work area as possible.

Methods for Estimating Materials	
Sand, gravel, topsoil (2" layer)	surface area (sq. ft.) ÷ 100 = tons needed
Standard brick pavers (4" × 8")	surface area (sq. ft.) × 5 = number of pavers needed
Poured concrete (4" layer)	surface area (sq. ft.) × .012 = cubic yards needed
Flagstone	surface area (sq. ft.) ÷ 100 = tons of stone needed
Interlocking block (6" × 16" face)	area of wall face (sq. ft.) × 1.5 = number of stones needed
Retaining wall timbers (5" × 6" × 8 ft.)	area of wall face (sq. ft.) ÷ 3 = number of timbers needed
Cut stone for 1-ft.-thick walls	area of wall face (sq. ft.) ÷ 15 = tons of stone needed
Rubble stone for 1 ft. thick walls	area of wall face (sq. ft.) ÷ 35 = tons of stone needed
8 × 8 × 16 concrete block for free-standing walls	height of wall (ft.) × length of wall × 1.125 = number of blocks

Using Landscape Professionals

Using landscape professionals can save work time and simplify large, complicated projects. Professional designers can help you plan and budget your project, and contractors can save you work time on large, difficult tasks.

The abilities and reputations of designers and contractors vary greatly, so always check references and insist on viewing samples of previous work before hiring a professional. Make sure to get a written, itemized estimate; terms for payment; and proof of bonding and insurance.

Landscape Professionals

Landscape architect: a licensed structural designer who is qualified to plan large, highly technical structures, like a tall retaining wall or free-standing garden wall, an in-ground swimming pool, or gazebo.

Landscape designer: a general-purpose design professional, often affiliated with a large nursery. Reputable landscape designers are the best choice for designing and planning help.

Garden designer: usually employed at a garden center or nursery. Garden designers can help you choose plants and plan gardening areas.

Landscape contractor: supplies workers and supervises labor for a wide range of landscaping projects. Landscaping contractors range from small one- and two-man crews to large, well-established companies that can oversee all stages of a landscape project.

Excavating contractor: provides labor and machinery required for large digging and excavation projects. Make sure utility companies locate and mark underground lines before the contractor begins work.

Concrete contractor: a specialized professional skilled at pouring and finishing concrete patios, driveways, sidewalks, steps, and walls.

Common supplies for landscape construction include: (A) sheet plastic, (B) landscape fabric, (C) burlap, (D) stucco lath, (E) bendable rigid plastic edging, (F) post caps, (G) wood sealer-preservative, (H) mason's string, (I) rigid plastic edging, (J) flexible plastic edging, (K) rope, (L) perforated drain pipe, (M) masonry sealer, (N) splash block for runoff water.

Landscaping Supplies

In addition to the visible design materials used in a landscape (pages 28 to 31), there are many hidden, structural supplies that are equally important to successful landscaping projects.

Because landscape structures are exposed to weather extremes, make sure to invest in the best materials you can afford. Buying cheap materials to save a few dollars can shorten the life span of a landscape structure by many years.

Metal connecting materials, including nails, screws, fence hardware, and post anchors should be made from aluminum or galvanized steel, which will not rust.

Check grade stamps on pressure-treated lumber. Look for lumber treated with chromated copper arsenate, identified by the "CCA" label printed on the grade stamp. For above-ground and ground-contact applications, choose lumber graded "LP-22" or ".40 retention." If wood will be buried, use lumber graded "FDN" or ".60 retention," if it is available.

Base materials for landscape walls and paved surfaces include: (A) sand, (B) seed gravel, (C) compactible gravel subbase containing a large amount of clay and lime, (D) topsoil, (E) coarse gravel, used as backfill, (F) mortar mix, and (G) concrete mix.

Connecting materials for landscape construction include: (A) galvanized common nails, (B) galvanized finish nails, (C) self-tapping masonry anchors, (D) galvanized utility screws, (E) 12" galvanized spikes, (F) concrete reinforcement bars, (G) lead masonry anchors, (H) metal pipes for anchoring timbers, (I) lag screws with washers, (J) construction adhesive, (K) J-bolts, (L) galvanized post anchor, (M) rafter strap, (N) fence bracket.

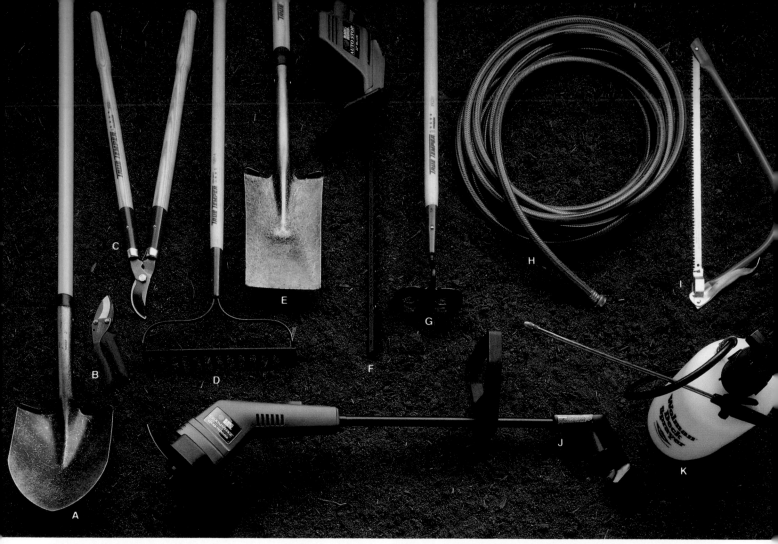

Basic yard and garden tools used in landscape construction and maintenance include: (A) garden shovel, (B) hand shears, (C) pruning shears, (D) garden rake, (E) spade, (F) power trimmer, (G) hoe, (H) garden hose, (I) bow saw, (J) line-feed trimmer, (K) pressure sprayer.

Tools for Landscape Construction

A sturdy wheelbarrow is an essential tool for landscape construction and maintenance. Better wheelbarrows have inflatable rubber tires and wooden handles.

Most landscape construction projects can be done with ordinary garden tools and workshop tools you already own. If you need to buy new tools, always invest in high-quality products. A few specialty tools, most of which can be borrowed or rented, make some jobs easier.

When using power tools outdoors, always use a GFCI (ground-fault circuit-interrupter) extension cord for safety. After each use, clean and dry metal tools to prevent rust.

Basic hand and power tools used in landscape construction include: (A) reciprocating saw, (B) hammer, (C) hand maul, (D) rubber mallet, (E) pencil, (F) circular saw, (G) eye protection, (H) drill with bits, (I) line level, (J) carpenter's level, (K) carpenter's square, (L) plumb bob and chalk line, (M) tape measures, (N) GFCI extension cord, (O) particle mask, (P) work gloves, (Q) caulk gun, (R) hearing protectors.

Specialty tools you can rent include: (A) tamping machine, (B) "jumping jack" tamping machine, (C) sod cutter, (D) power auger, (E) hand tamper, (F) chain saw.

Tools for masonry work include: (A) mortar bag, (B) masonry chisel, (C) V-shaped mortar tool, (D) stiff broom, (E) masonry drill bits, (F) concrete float, (G) pointed trowel, (H) standard trowel, (I) rubber gloves, (J) masonry saw blade.

Landscape
Construction
Projects

Build contours to create visual interest in a flat landscape. Contours should have gentle slopes and irregular shapes that accent the surrounding yard. Contours can be used to create a visual barrier, or to provide planting areas (pages 122 to 123).

Grading & Contouring Your Yard

Reshaping, removing, or adding soil is an important step in many landscaping projects. If you are installing a patio, for example, you may need to first create a large area that is very flat. Or you may want to put a finishing touch on a landscape by adding raised contours or planting areas to the yard.

Consider how the overall slope affects drainage in your yard. Make sure your finished landscape is graded so it directs runoff water away from buildings and minimizes low-lying areas that can trap standing water. To identify drainage problems, examine your yard immediately after a heavy rain, or after watering it thoroughly, and look for areas where water collects or flows toward building foundations.

Before digging, contact utility companies to pinpoint and mark the location of underground wires or pipes. You can arrange to have utility lines rerouted if there is no way to work around them.

Everything You Need:

Tools: hose, shovel, tape measure, garden rake, wheelbarrow, hammer or maul, line level.

Materials (as needed): edging material, topsoil, gravel, string, stakes, perforated drain pipe, splash block, sod, landscape fabric.

Hire an excavating contractor if you need to move large amounts of soil. Small front-end loaders are available for daily rental, but using them successfully requires some practice.

How to Create a Landscape Contour

1 Create an outline of the planned contour on your lawn, using a hose or rope. If the contour will be used as a planting area, install edging material along the outline.

2 Fill the outlined area with topsoil. Use a rake to shape the soil into a smooth mound no more than 18" high, then tamp and water the soil to compress it. Landscape contours can be finished with sod or used as planting areas (pages 122 to 123).

How to Grade Soil Around Foundations

Prevent water damage to foundations by grading soil so there is a smooth, gradual slope away from the building. For proper drainage, the ground within 6 ft. of a foundation should drop 3/4" for each foot of distance. To check the grade, attach a string to a pair of stakes and adjust the string so it is level. Measure down from the string at 1-ft. intervals to determine the grade. If necessary, add extra soil and shape it with a garden rake to get the proper grade.

Tips for Solving Drainage Problems

Drainage
swale

Fill small low-lying areas by top-dressing them with black soil. Spread the new soil into an even layer, then compress it with a hand tamper.

Improve drainage in a large low-lying area by creating a shallow ditch, called a drainage swale, to carry runoff water away. If your region receives frequent heavy rainfalls, or if you have dense soil that drains poorly, you may need to lay a perforated drain pipe and a bed of gravel under the swale to make it more effective (page opposite).

How to Make a Drainage Swale

Swale
route

1 After identifying the problem area, use stakes to mark a swale route that will direct water away from the site toward a runoff area. The outlet of the swale must be lower than any point in the problem area.

2 Dig a 6"-deep, rounded trench along the swale route. If you remove the sod carefully, you can lay it back into the trench when the swale is completed.

3 Shape the trench so it slopes gradually downward toward the outlet, and the sides and bottom are smooth.

4 Complete the swale by laying sod into the trench. Compress the sod, then water the area thoroughly to check the drainage.

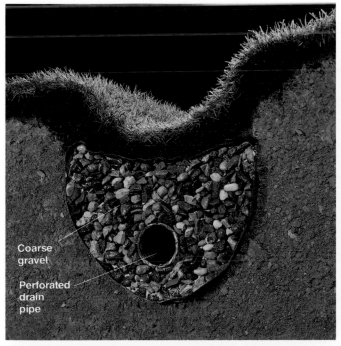

Coarse gravel

Perforated drain pipe

Splash block

OPTION: For severe drainage problems, dig a 1-ft.-deep swale angled slightly downward to the outlet point. Line the swale with landscape fabric. Spread a 2" layer of coarse gravel in the bottom of the swale, then lay perforated drain pipe over the gravel. Cover the pipe with a 5" layer of gravel, then wrap the landscape fabric over the top of the gravel. Cover the swale with soil and fresh sod. Set a splash block at the outlet to distribute the runoff and prevent erosion.

Cut stone is a top-quality, expensive building material used for retaining walls (shown above) and free-standing garden walls. For retaining walls, cut stone is laid without mortar to improve drainage, except for the top row, which can be anchored with mortar for extra strength. Retaining wall designs often include garden steps. For free-standing garden walls, cut stones usually are mortared. When built correctly, cut-stone walls can last for generations. See pages 64 to 65.

Landscape Walls

Landscape walls include retaining walls and free-standing walls. They can define outdoor areas, increase the amount of level yard area, stop soil erosion, and improve the appearance of your yard and home.

Many stone, concrete, and wood products can be used to build landscape walls. When choosing materials, consider style, cost, ease of installation, and durability. Refer to pages 28 to 31 for more information on materials commonly used in landscape construction.

Wherever possible, limit the height of your landscape walls to 3 ft. Local Building Codes usually require deep concrete footings and special construction techniques for taller landscape walls.

Retaining walls are subject to enormous pressure from the weight of the soil behind the wall. To offset this pressure, build the retaining wall so each row of materials is set slightly behind the previous row. The backward angle of a retaining wall (at least 1" for every foot in height) is called the "batter." For maximum strength, some landscape contractors tilt the entire wall back into the hillside.

Common Materials Used for Landscape Walls

Landscape timbers are inexpensive and easy to cut at any angle, but are less durable than stone or masonry. A well-built timber retaining wall made with good-quality pressure-treated lumber will last for 15 to 20 years in most climates. See pages 62 to 63.

Rubble stone is used for both retaining walls and free-standing garden walls, and usually is laid without mortar. Building rubble-stone walls requires patience, but the materials are less expensive than cut stone or interlocking block. See page 64.

Interlocking block made from cast concrete is the easiest of all materials to work with. It makes very strong and durable retaining walls, and is less expensive than cut stone. Interlocking block is especially useful for curved retaining walls. See pages 59 to 61.

Concrete block is inexpensive and is available in decorative and plain styles. Concrete block requires mortar, and makes a very sturdy free-standing garden wall. But because the mortared joints hinder drainage, concrete block is a poor choice for retaining walls. See pages 66 to 71.

Terraced retaining walls work well on steep hillsides. Two or more short retaining walls are easier to install and more stable than a single, tall retaining wall. Construct the terraces so each wall is no higher than 3 ft.

Building a Retaining Wall

The main reason to build retaining walls is to create level planting areas or prevent erosion on hillsides. But if you have a flat yard, you also can build low retaining wall structures to make decorative raised planting beds and add visual interest to the landscape.

No matter what material is used, a retaining wall can be damaged if water saturates the soil behind it. To ensure its durability, make sure your wall contains the proper drainage features (page opposite).

Retaining walls taller than 3 ft. are subject to thousands of pounds of pressure from the weight of the soil and water, so they require special building techniques that are best left to a professional. If you have a tall hillside, it is best to terrace the hill with several short walls (photo, above).

Before excavating for a retaining wall, **check with local utility companies** to make sure there are no underground pipes or cables running through the site.

Everything You Need for Retaining Walls:

Tools: wheelbarrow, shovel, garden rake, line level, hand tamper, rented tamping machine, small maul, masonry chisel, eye protection, hearing protectors, work gloves, circular saw, level, tape measure, marking pencil.

Materials: stakes, mason's string, landscape fabric, compactible gravel subbase, perforated drain pipe, coarse backfill gravel.

Added supplies for interlocking block walls: masonry blade for circular saw, caulk gun, construction adhesive.

Added supplies for stone walls: masonry chisel, masonry blade for circular saw, trowel, mortar mix.

Added supplies for timber walls: chain saw or reciprocating saw, drill and 1" spade bit, 12" galvanized spikes.

Options for Positioning a Retaining Wall

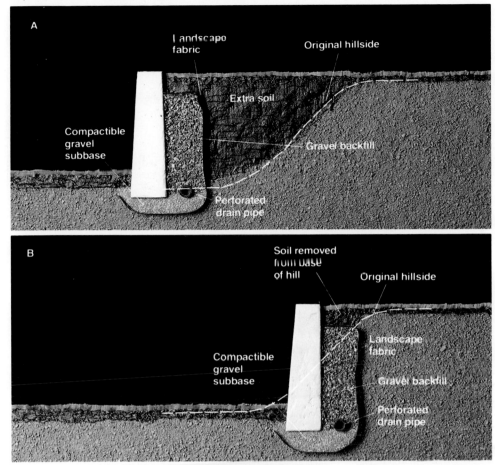

(A) Increase the level area above the wall by positioning the wall well forward from the top of the hill. Fill in behind the wall with extra soil, available from sand-and-gravel companies.

(B) Keep the basic shape of your yard by positioning the wall near the top of the hillside. Use the soil removed at the base of the hill to fill in near the top of the wall.

Structural features for all retaining walls include: a compactible gravel sub-base to make a solid footing for the wall, coarse gravel backfill and a perforated drain pipe to improve drainage behind the wall, and landscape fabric to keep the loose soil from washing into the gravel backfill.

Providing Drainage for Retaining Walls

Backfill with gravel and install a perforated drain pipe near the bottom of the gravel backfill. Vent the pipe to the side or bottom of the retaining wall, where runoff water can flow away from the hillside without causing erosion.

Dig a swale, a shallow ditch 1 ft. to 2 ft. away from the top of the wall, to direct runoff water away from the retaining wall (see pages 52 to 53). This technique is useful for sites that have very dense soil that does not drain well.

How to Prepare a Retaining Wall Site

1 Excavate the hillside, if necessary, to create a level base for the retaining wall. For interlocking blocks or stone walls, allow at least 12" of space for gravel backfill between the back of the wall and the hillside. For timber walls, allow at least 3 ft. of space. When excavating large areas, rent earth-moving equipment or hire a contractor.

2 Use stakes to mark the front edge of the wall at the ends and at any corners and curves. Connect the stakes with mason's string. Use a line level to check the string, and, if necessary, adjust the string so it is level.

3 Dig a trench for the first row of building materials, measuring down from the mason's string to maintain a level trench. Make the trench 6" deeper than the thickness of one layer of building material. For example, if you are using 6"-thick interlocking blocks, make the trench 12" deep.

4 Line the excavation with strips of landscape fabric cut 3 ft. longer than the planned height of the wall. Make sure seams overlap by at least 6".

Building a Retaining Wall Using Interlocking Block

Several styles of interlocking block are available at building and outdoor centers. Most types have a natural rock finish that combines the rough texture of cut stone with the uniform shape and size of concrete blocks.

Interlocking blocks weigh up to 80 lbs. each, so it is a good idea to have helpers when building a retaining wall. Suppliers offer substantial discounts when interlocking block is purchased in large quantities, so you may be able to save money if you coordinate your own project with those of your neighbors.

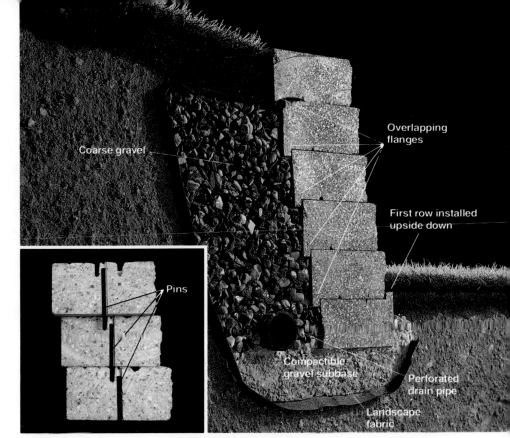

Interlocking wall blocks do not need mortar. Some types are held together with a system of overlapping flanges that automatically set the backward angle (batter) as the blocks are stacked. Other types of blocks use a pinning system (inset).

Tips for Building a Retaining Wall Using Interlocking Block

Make a stepped trench when the ends of a retaining wall must blend into an existing hillside. Retaining walls often are designed so the ends curve or turn back into the slope.

Make half-blocks by scoring full blocks with a circular saw and masonry blade, then breaking the blocks along the scored line with a maul and chisel. Half-blocks are used when making corners, and to ensure that vertical joints between blocks are staggered between rows.

1 Spread a 6" layer of compactible gravel subbase into the trench and pack thoroughly. A rented tamping machine, sometimes called a "jumping jack," works better than a hand tamper (step 7) for packing the subbase.

2 Lay the first row of blocks into the trench, aligning the front edges with the mason's string. When using flanged blocks, place the first row of blocks upside down and backward. Check the blocks frequently with a level, and adjust, if necessary, by adding or removing subbase material below the blocks.

3 Lay the second row of blocks according to manufacturer's instructions. On flanged blocks, the blocks should be laid so the flanges are tight against the underlying blocks. Check regularly to make sure the blocks are level.

4 Add 6" of gravel behind the blocks, making sure the landscape fabric remains between the gravel and the hillside. Pack the gravel thoroughly with a hand tamper.

5 Place perforated drain pipe on top of the gravel, at least 6" behind wall, with perforations facing down. Make sure that at least one end of the pipe is unobstructed so runoff water can escape (page 57). Lay additional rows of blocks until the wall is about 18" above ground level. Make sure the vertical joints in adjoining rows are offset.

6 Fill behind the wall with coarse gravel, and pack well. Lay the remaining rows of block, except for the cap row, backfilling with gravel and packing with a hand tamper as you go.

7 Before laying the cap blocks, fold the end of the landscape fabric over the gravel backfill. Add a thin layer of topsoil over the fabric, then pack it thoroughly with a hand tamper.

8 Fold any excess landscape fabric back over the soil, then apply construction adhesive to the blocks. Lay the cap blocks in place. Use topsoil to fill in behind the wall and to fill in the trench at the base of the wall. Install sod or other plants, as desired.

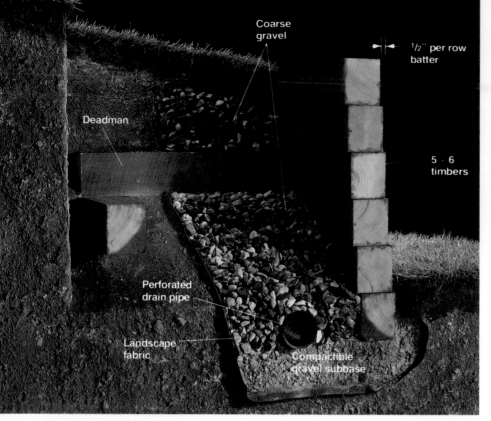

Coarse gravel

Deadman

Perforated drain pipe

Landscape fabric

Compactible gravel subbase

1/2" per row batter

5 · 6 timbers

Building a Retaining Wall Using Timbers

Timber walls have a life span of 15 to 20 years if built correctly. Use pressure-treated timbers at least 5 × 6 in size. Smaller timbers are not sturdy enough for retaining walls.

Use a chain saw or a reciprocating saw to cut landscape timbers. The pesticides used in treated lumber are toxic, so wear a particle mask, gloves, and long sleeves when cutting or handling pressure-treated lumber. Avoid using old timbers, like discarded railroad ties, that have been soaked in creosote. Creosote can leach into the soil and kill plants.

Before building the retaining wall, prepare the site as directed on page 58.

Timber retaining walls must be anchored with "deadmen" that extend from the wall back into the soil. Deadmen prevent the wall from sagging under the weight of the soil. For best results with timber retaining walls, create a backward angle (batter) by setting each row of timbers 1/2" behind the preceding row. The first row of timbers should be buried.

Tips for Strengthening a Timber Retaining Wall

Use metal reinforcement bars instead of spikes for extra strength when connecting timbers. Cut 12" to 24" lengths of bar with sharp points, then drive them into pilot holes drilled through the top timber, spaced at 2-ft. intervals. This technique is especially useful if you have heavy, dense soil that drains poorly.

Timber depth equal to 1/2 exposed height

Install vertical anchor posts to reinforce the wall. Space the posts 3 ft. apart, and install them so the buried depth of each post is at least half the exposed height of the wall. Anchor posts are essential if it is not practical to install deadmen (photo, top).

How to Build a Retaining Wall Using Timbers

1 Spread a 6" layer of compactible gravel subbase into the prepared trench, then tamp the subbase and begin laying timbers, following the same techniques as with interlocking blocks (steps 1 to 7, pages 60 to 61). Each row of timbers should be set with a 1/2" batter, and end joints should be staggered so they do not align.

2 Use 12" galvanized spikes or reinforcement bars to anchor the ends of each timber to the underlying timbers. Stagger the ends of the timbers to form strong corner joints. Drive additional spikes along the length of the timbers at 2-ft. intervals. If you have trouble driving the spikes, drill pilot holes.

3 Install deadmen, spaced 4 ft. apart, midway up the wall. Build the deadmen by joining 3-ft.-long lengths of timber with 12" spikes, then insert the ends through holes cut in the landscape fabric. Anchor deadmen to wall with spikes. Install the remaining rows of timbers, and finish backfilling behind the wall (steps 6 to 8, page 61).

4 Improve drainage by drilling weep holes through the second row of landscape timbers and into the gravel backfill, using a spade bit. Space the holes 4 ft. apart, and angle them upward.

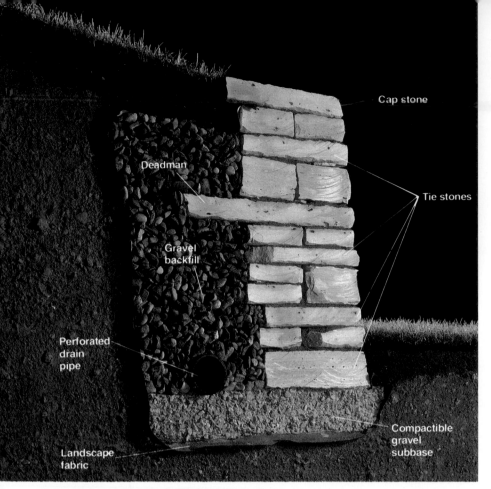

Building a Retaining Wall Using Natural Stone

Retaining walls made from natural cut stone or rubble stone give a traditional, timeless look to a landscape. Natural stone walls usually are laid without mortar, although the last one or two rows can be mortared in place for greater strength. Unlike mortared stone or block walls (pages 66 to 71), unmortared stone walls require no concrete footings.

Before building the retaining wall, prepare the site as directed on page 58. Build the wall by placing the largest stones at the bottom and reserving the smoothest, flattest stones for the corners and the top (cap) row.

Cut stone has flat, smooth surfaces for easy stacking. For a stable retaining wall, alternate rows of "tie stones" that span the entire width of the wall with rows of smaller stones. Install extra-long stones (called deadmen) that extend back into gravel backfill, spaced every 4 to 6 ft.

Retaining Wall Variations Using Rubble Stone

Boulders are large, uncut rocks, usually round in shape. The retaining wall site requires no subbase or backfill: simply dig out the hillside to fit the shape of the boulders and roll them into place. Boulders range in size from about 40 lbs. to several hundred lbs. For heavy boulders, you may want to hire a contractor to deliver and position the rocks.

Field stone refers to any irregular assortment of rough rock. You can gather field stone by hand or buy it from sand-and-gravel companies. Field-stone retaining walls do not need a subbase or backfill; but for better stability, build the wall so it tilts back into the hillside. Pack the open spaces between rocks with rock fragments or soil. If you wish, plant vines or groundcover in the exposed gaps.

64

How to Build a Retaining Wall Using Cut Stone

1 Spread a 6" layer of compactible gravel subbase into the prepared trench (step 1, page 60), then sort the stones by size and shape so they can be located easily as you build. Make sure you have enough long stones to serve as tie stones, dead-men, and cap stones.

2 Trim irregular stones, if needed, to make them fit solidly into the wall. Always wear eye protection and hearing protectors when cutting stone. Score the stone first using a masonry blade and circular saw set to 1/8" blade depth, then drive a masonry chisel along the scored line until the stone breaks.

Tie stone

Dead man

3 Lay rows of stones, following the same techniques for backfilling as for interlocking blocks (steps 2 to 7, pages 60 to 61). Build a backward slant (batter) into the wall by setting each row of stones about 1/2" back from the preceding row. For stability, work tie stones and deadmen into the wall at frequent intervals.

Cap stone

4 Before laying the cap row of stones, mix mortar according to manufacturer's directions and apply a thick bed along the tops of the installed stones, keeping the mortar at least 6" from the front face of the wall. Lay the cap stones, and press them into the mortar. Because the mortar is not visible, this technique is called "blind mortaring." Finish backfilling behind the wall (step 8, page 61).

Building a Free-standing Wall

A free-standing wall serves the same function as a hedge or fence, but is much sturdier. Walls are popular in areas where growing shrubs and hedges is difficult. Free-standing walls can train climbing plants or support trellises or container plants. Low walls may be used as garden benches.

Most free-standing walls are built by mortaring concrete block, brick, or natural stone. The following pages show how to build a concrete block wall, but similar techniques can be used for any mortared wall.

Free-standing walls also can be built from unmortared stones, using techniques similar to those used in building a stone retaining wall (pages 64 to 65).

Limit your walls to 3 ft. in height. Taller walls need deep footings and extra reinforcement. Increase privacy by adding a trellis to the wall (photo, top left). Many local Building Codes limit the total height of the wall and trellis to 6 ft.

A stucco finish and lattice panels turn a plain concrete block wall into a durable, attractive privacy wall. See pages 72 to 73 for these finishing techniques.

Everything You Need:

Tools: tape measure, rake, hammer, level, shovel, wheelbarrow, old paint brush, chalk line, trowel, rubber gloves, pencil, line level, masonry chisel, masonry hammer, V-shaped mortar tool, garden hoe, level.

Materials: rope, stakes, 2 × 6 lumber, compactible gravel subbase, reinforcement rods, oil, premixed concrete, concrete blocks, sheet plastic, 3/8"-thick wood strips, mortar mix, mason's string.

Other Options for Finishing a Concrete Block Wall

Stone veneer (sometimes called cultured stone) copies the look of natural stone at a fraction of the cost. Available in dozens of different styles, stone veneer kits come with an assortment of flat pieces and corner pieces. The veneer is held in place with a layer of standard mortar (page 73).

Decorative block adds visual interest to a plain concrete block wall. Check with your local building inspector before adding block to a wall, since the added height may require extra reinforcement. Decorative block also may be used to build an entire wall (page 55).

How to Install a Footing for a Free-standing Wall

1 Lay out the rough position of the wall, using a rope.

2 Outline the wall footing, using stakes and mason's string. Check the string with a linc level and adjust as needed. The footing should be twice as wide as the planned wall, and should extend 1 ft. beyond each end.

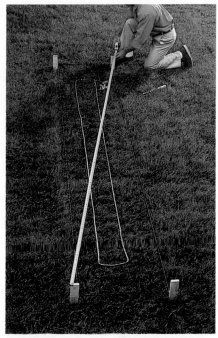

3 Measure the diagonals to make sure the outline is square, and adjust as necessary. Dig a 1-ft.-deep trench for the footing, using the strings as a guide. Make sure the bottom of the trench is roughly level.

4 Lay a 6" layer of compactible gravel subbase into the trench. Tamp the subbase thoroughly (page 61). NOTE: Follow local Building Code guidelines for footing depth.

5 Build a wood form using 2 × 6 lumber, and set it in the trench. Add or remove subbase material to level the form. Drive stakes along the outside of the form to anchor it.

6 Lay reinforcement bars inside the form to make the footing more crack-resistant. Set the bars on 2 × 4 scraps, a few inches inside the form. Coat the inside of the form with oil for easy removal.

(continued next page)

7 Fill the form up to the top of the boards with concrete. Work the concrete with a shovel just enough to remove air pockets.

8 Smooth off (screed) the surface of the concrete by dragging a short 2 × 4 along the top of the form. Add concrete to any low areas, and screed again.

9 When concrete is hard to the touch, cover it with plastic and let it cure for 2 or 3 days. When surface has cured, pry the forms loose with a shovel.

How to Build a Free-standing Wall Using Concrete Block

 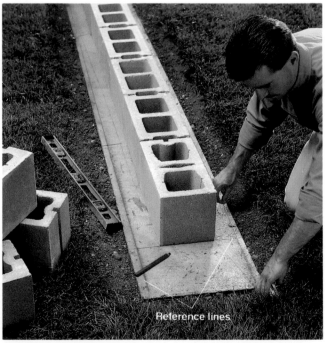

Reference lines

1 Test-fit a row of blocks on the footing, using smooth-sided end blocks at the ends. You may need to use half-blocks on one end to achieve the desired wall length. Use 3/8"-thick wood strips or dowels as spacers to maintain an even gap for mortar between the blocks.

2 Draw pencil lines on the concrete to mark the ends of the test-fitted row. Extend the line well past the edges of the block. Use a chalk line to snap reference lines on each side of the footing, 3" from the blocks. These reference lines will serve as a guide when setting the blocks into mortar.

3 Remove the blocks and set them nearby. Mix mortar in a wheelbarrow or large pail, following manufacturer's directions. Mortar should be moist enough to hold its shape when squeezed.

4 Trowel thick lines of mortar, slightly wider and longer than the base of the end block, onto the center of the footing. If the footing has cured for over a week, dampen it before mortaring.

Wider flanges

TIP: When positioning concrete blocks, make sure the side with the wider flanges is facing upward. The wider flanges provide more surface for applying mortar.

5 Set an end block into the mortar, so the end is aligned with the pencil mark on the footing. Set a level on top of the block, then tap the block with a trowel handle until it is level. Use the chalkline as a reference point for keeping the block in line.

6 Apply mortar, then set and level the block at the opposite end of the footing. Stake a mason's string even with the top outside corners of the blocks. Check the string with a line level, then adjust the blocks to align with the string. Remove excess mortar, and fill the gaps beneath the end blocks (inset).

(continued next page)

7 Apply mortar to the vertical flanges on one side of a standard block (inset) and to the footing, using a trowel. Set the block next to the end block, leaving a 3/8" layer of mortar between blocks. Tap the block into position with a trowel handle, using the string as a guide to align the block.

8 Install the remaining blocks, working back and forth from opposite ends. Be careful to maintain 3/8" joints to ensure that the last block in the row will fit. Make sure the row is level and straight by aligning the blocks with the mason's string and checking them with a carpenter's level.

9 At the middle of the row, apply mortar to the vertical flanges on both sides of the last block, then slide the block down into place. Align the last block with the mason's string.

10 Apply a 1" layer of mortar to the top flanges of the end blocks. Scrape off any mortar that falls onto the footing.

11 Begin laying the second row. Use half-size end blocks to create staggered vertical joints. Check with a straightedge to make sure the new blocks are aligned with the bottom blocks.

VARIATION: If your wall has a corner, begin the second row with a full-sized end block that spans the vertical joint formed where two sides of the wall meet. This creates staggered vertical joints.

12 Insert a nail into the wet mortar at each end of the wall. Attach a mason's string to one nail, then stretch the string up over the corners of the end blocks and tie it to the nail at the opposite end.

13 Install the second row of blocks, using the same method as with the first row. When the second row is completed, remove the nails and mason's string. Scrape off excess mortar, and finish the joints with a V-shaped mortar tool. (If you will be stuccoing the wall, finish the joints flush with the block.) Install each additional row of blocks by repeating steps 11 to 13. Finish the joints as each row of blocks is completed.

14 Complete the wall with a row of cap blocks. Cap blocks are very heavy, and must be laid gently to keep mortar from being squeezed out. If you are adding lattice panels to the top of the wall, insert J-bolts into the joints between the cap blocks while mortar is still wet (page 72).

How to Add Lattice Panels to a Block Wall

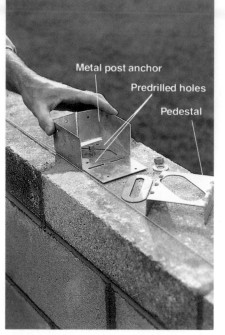

Metal post anchor

Predrilled holes

Pedestal

1 While mortar is still wet, install 3/8"-diameter J-bolts into the center of the cap row joints at post locations. About 1" of the bolt should protrude. Pack mortar around the bolt and let it harden. (If mortar already has hardened, see OPTION, step 2.)

2 Align and attach a metal post anchor at each post location. Slip an oval washer over each J-bolt, then attach a nut. OPTION: Attach metal post anchors by driving self-tapping masonry anchors through the predrilled holes in the bottom of the post anchor.

3 Set a metal pedestal into each anchor. The top of the J-bolt should be below the pedestal.

4 Cut a 4 × 4 post for each anchor. Set the post on the pedestal, then bend the open flange up against the post. Make sure the post is plumb, then attach it with 6d galvanized nails.

5 Assemble and install lattice panels between posts, as directed on pages 113. Most lattice panels are 8 ft. long, and can be cut to fit if your posts are spaced less than 8 ft. apart.

How to Finish a Block Wall with Stucco

1 Mix stucco for the base coat, following the manufacturer's directions. Apply a ⅜"-thick layer over the block, using a square-end trowel and working from the bottom up.

2 Scratch the base coat with a V-notched tool or plaster rake to create a rough surface for the finish coat to bond with. Let the base coat cure for two days, dampening the stucco with water a few times daily.

3 Apply a finish coat of stucco in a smooth, ¼"-thick layer, using the trowel, then texture the surface with a float covered with carpet. Let the stucco cure for two days, dampening a few times daily.

Variation: Apply a wet-dash finish by flinging, or *dashing,* stucco over the finish coat, using a wisk broom.

Variation: Create a knock-down finish by applying stucco using the wet-dash technique, then flattening the peaks with a trowel.

How to Apply Stone Veneer to a Block Wall

1 Prepare wall with wire lath (step 1, above), then apply a ¹/₂"-thick layer of standard mortar to the wall. Scratch grooves into the damp mortar, using the trowel tip, then allow to dry overnight. Beginning at the bottom of the wall, apply mortar to the back of each veneer piece, then press it onto the wall with a twisting motion. Keep a ¹/₂" gap between pieces.

2 After mortar has dried for a day, fill the joints with fresh mortar, using a mortar bag. Use a V-shaped mortar tool to finish the joints (step 13, page 71).

Flagstone walkways combine charm with durability, and work well in both casual and formal settings. Also a popular material for patios, flagstone can be set in sand, or it can be mortared in place. See pages 78 to 79. TIP: Prevent damage to the edging material by trimming near the walkway with a line-feed trimmer insead of a mower.

Building Walkways & Paths

Walkways and paths serve as "hallways" between heavily used areas of your yard, and can be used to direct traffic toward a favorite landscape feature, like a pond. Walkways also create a visual corridor that directs the eye from one area to another.

Curved paths give a softer, more relaxed look to a landscape, but straight or angular paths and walkways fit well in contemporary landscape designs.

Garden paths often are made from loose materials, like crushed rock or bark, held in place by edging. Walkways are more durable when made from stone or brick paving materials set in sand or mortar. Poured concrete sidewalks are practical and the most durable, but unless you have a lot of experience pouring and curing concrete, do not attempt to build them yourself. Most paving techniques used in patio construction (pages 90 to 99) can be used for walkways as well.

Everything You Need:

Tools: tape measure, spade, garden rake, rubber mallet, circular saw with masonry blade, masonry chisel, masonry hammer.

Materials: landscape fabric, garden hose, edging material (page 76), walkway surface materials, galvanized screws, 2 x 6 lumber. Added supplies for mortared brick walkways: mortar, mortar bag, V-shaped mortar tool, trowel.

Loose materials, such as gravel, crushed rock, wood chips and bark, make informal, inexpensive pathways that are well suited for light-traffic areas. Build loose-material paths with the surface material slightly above ground level, to keep it from being washed away.

Brick pavers provide stately charm to a main walkway, making a house more appealing from the street. Because pavers are very durable, they are ideal for heavy-traffic areas. Brick pavers can be set in sand, or mortared in place over an old concrete surface. Pavers used for mortared walkways often are thinner than those designed for sand installation.

Tips for Building a Walkway

Use a sod cutter to strip grass from your pathway site. Available at most rental centers, sod cutters excavate to a very even depth. The cut sod can be replanted in other parts of your lawn.

Install stakes and strings when laying out straight walkways made from stone paving materials, and measure from the strings to ensure straight sides and uniform excavation depth.

Brick edging makes a good boundary for both straight and curved paths made from loose materials. See page 77.

Wood edging makes a sturdy border for straight walkways made from flagstone or brick pavers set in sand. See pages 78 to 79.

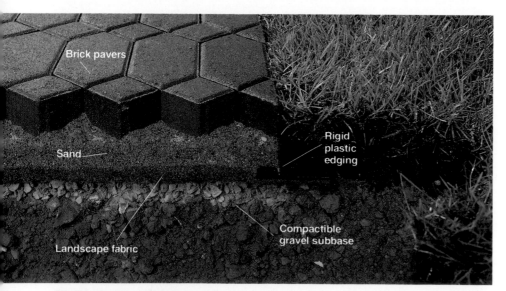

Rigid plastic edging installs easily, and works well for both curved and straight walkways made from paving stones or brick pavers set in sand. See pages 90 to 99.

Types of Edging

Use edging to keep walkway materials in place. Consider cost, appearance, flexibility, and ease of installation when selecting an edging type.

Brick edging set in soil is good for casual, lightly traveled pathways, but should be used only in soil that is dense and well drained. (Bricks in loose or swampy soil will not hold their position). Bricks can be set vertically, or tilted at an angle to make a saw-tooth pattern. Brick pavers also can be mortared to the sides of an old sidewalk to create a border for a new surface (pages 80 to 81).

Wood edging made from pressure-treated lumber, redwood, or cedar is inexpensive and easy to install. The tops of the boards are left exposed to create an attractive border. The wood edging boards are held in place by attaching them to recessed wood stakes spaced every 12" along the outside of the edging.

Rigid plastic edging is inconspicuous, durable, and easy to install. It was developed as an edging for brick pavers set in sand. Rigid plastic edging is held in place by the weight of the soil and with galvanized spikes driven through the back flange. Rolled vinyl edging is used most often to make boundaries for planting areas (pages 122 to 123), but also works as an edging for casual walkways. It is inexpensive and very flexible.

How to Build a Path Using Loose Materials & Brick Edging

1 Outline the path using a garden hose or rope (page 38), then excavate the site to a depth of 2" to 3", using a spade, hoe, or a rented sod cutter (page 75). Rake the site smooth.

2 Dig narrow edging trenches about 2" deeper than the path site along both edges of the excavation, using a spade or hoe.

3 Lay landscaping fabric between the edging trenches to prevent weeds from growing. Overlap sheets by at least 6".

4 Set bricks on end into the edging trenches, with the tops slightly above ground level. Pack soil behind and beneath each brick, adjusting the bricks, if necessary, to keep the rows even.

5 Finish the path by spreading loose material (gravel, crushed rock, bark, or wood chips) between the rows of edging bricks. Level the surface with a garden rake. The loose material should be slightly above ground level. Tap each brick lightly on the inside face to help set it into the soil. Inspect and adjust the bricks yearly, adding new loose material as needed.

How to Build a Flagstone Walkway Using Wood Edging

1 Outline the walkway site and excavate to a depth of 6". Allow enough room for the edging and stakes (step 2). For straight walkways, use stakes and strings to maintain a uniform outline (page 75). Add a 2" layer of compactible gravel subbase, using a rake to smooth the surface.

2 Install 2 × 6 edging made from pressure-treated lumber around the sides of the site. Drive 12" stakes on the outside of the edging, spaced 12" apart. Tops of the stakes should be below ground level. Attach the edging to the stakes using galvanized screws.

3 Test-fit the flagstones to find an efficient, attractive arrangement of stones. Arrange the stones to minimize the number of cuts needed. Leave a gap between stones that is at least 3/8", but no more than 2" wide. Use a pencil to mark stones for cutting, then remove the stones and set them nearby.

4 Cut flagstones by scoring along the marked lines with a circular saw and masonry blade set to 1/8" blade depth. Set a piece of wood under the stone, just inside the scored line, then use a masonry chisel and hammer to strike along the scored line until the stone breaks.

Flagstone thickness

Width of walkway

5 Lay sheets of landscape fabric over the walkway site to prevent plants and grass from growing up between the stones. (Omit the landscape fabric if you want to plant grass or ground cover to fill the cracks.) Spread a 2" layer of sand over the land-scape fabric to serve as the base for the flagstones.

6 Make a "screed" for smoothing the sand by notching the ends of a short 2 x 6 to fit inside the edging (see inset). The depth of the notches should equal the thickness of the stones, usually about 2". Screed the base by pulling the 2 x 6 from one end of the walkway to the other. Add more sand as needed until the base is smooth.

7 Beginning at one corner of the walkway, lay the flagstones onto the sand base so the gap be-tween stones is at least 3/8", but no more than 2". If needed, add or remove sand beneath stones to level them. Set the stones by tapping them with a rubber mallet or a length of 2 x 4.

8 Fill the gaps between stones with sand. (Use soil if you are planting grass or ground cover in the cracks.) Pack the sand with your fingers or a piece of scrap wood, then spray the walkway lightly with water to help the sand settle. Add new sand as necessary until gaps are filled.

How to Resurface a Sidewalk Using Mortared Brick Pavers

1 Select a paver pattern (page 91), then dig a trench around the concrete, slightly wider than the thickness of one paver. Dig the trench so it is about 3 1/2" below the concrete surface. Soak the pavers with water before mortaring. Dry pavers absorb moisture, weakening the mortar strength.

2 Sweep the old concrete, then hose off the surface and sides with water to clear away dirt and debris. Mix a small batch of mortar according to manufacturer's directions. For convenience, place the mortar on a scrap of plywood.

3 Install edging bricks by applying a 1/2" layer of mortar to the side of the concrete slab and to one side of each brick. Set bricks into the trench, against the concrete. Brick edging should be 1/2" higher than the thickness of the brick pavers.

4 Finish the joints on the edging bricks with a V-shaped mortar tool (step 9), then mix and apply a 1/2"-thick bed of mortar to one end of the sidewalk, using a trowel. Mortar hardens very quickly, so work in sections no larger than 4 sq. ft.

5 Make a "screed" for smoothing mortar by notching the ends of a short 2 × 4 to fit between the edging bricks (page 79). Depth of the notches should equal the thickness of the pavers. Drag the screed across the mortar bed until the mortar is smooth.

6 Lay the paving bricks one at a time into the mortar, maintaining a 1/2" gap between pavers. (A piece of scrap plywood works well as a spacing guide.) Set the pavers by tapping them lightly with a rubber mallet.

7 As each section of pavers is completed, check with a straightedge to make sure the tops of the pavers are even.

8 When all the pavers are installed, use a mortar bag to fill the joints between the pavers with fresh mortar. Work in 4-sq.-ft. sections, and avoid getting mortar on the tops of the pavers.

9 Use a V-shaped mortar tool to finish the joints as you complete each 4-sq.-ft. section. For best results, finish the longer joints first, then the shorter joints. Use a trowel to remove excess mortar.

10 Let the mortar dry for a few hours, then scrub the pavers with a coarse rag and water. Cover the walkway with plastic and let the mortar cure for at least 24 hours. Remove plastic, but do not walk on the pavers for at least three days.

Simple garden steps can be built by making a series of concrete platforms framed with 5 × 6 timbers. Garden steps have shorter vertical risers and deeper horizontal treads than house stairs. Risers for garden stairs should be no more than 6", and treads should be at least 11" deep.

Building Garden Steps

Garden steps make sloping yards safer and more accessible. They also add visual interest by introducing new combinations of materials into your landscape design.

You can build garden steps with a wide variety of materials, including flagstone, brick, timbers, concrete block, or poured concrete. Whatever materials you use, make sure the steps are level and firmly anchored. They should be easy to climb and have a rough texture for good traction.

Everything You Need:

Tools: chain saw or reciprocating saw with 12" wood-cutting blade, tape measure, level, masonry hammer, shovel, drill with 1" spade bit and bit extension, rake, wheelbarrow, hoe, concrete float, edging tool, stiff brush.

Materials: 2 × 4 lumber, 5 × 6 landscape timbers, mason's string, 3/4" I.D. (interior diameter) black pipe, 12" galvanized spikes, premixed concrete, compactible gravel subbase, seed gravel (1/2" maximum diameter), sheet plastic, burlap.

Tips for Mixing Concrete

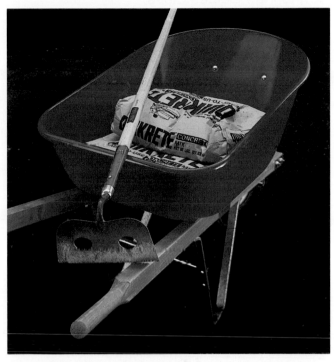

For large amounts (more than 1/2 cubic yard), mix your own dry ingredients in a wheelbarrow or rented mixer. Use a ratio of 1 part portland cement (A), 2 parts sand (B), and 3 parts gravel (C). See page 43 to estimate the amount of concrete needed.

For small amounts (less than 1/2 cubic yard), buy premixed bags of dry concrete. A 60-lb. bag of concrete creates about 1/2 cubic foot of concrete. A special hoe with holes in the blade is useful for mixing concrete.

Tips for Building Garden Steps

1/8" downward pitch per foot

Build a slight downward pitch into outdoor steps so water will drain off without puddling. Do not exceed a pitch of 1/8" per foot.

Order custom-cut timbers to reduce installation time if the dimensions of each step are identical. Some building supply centers charge a small fee for custom-cutting timbers.

How to Plan Garden Steps

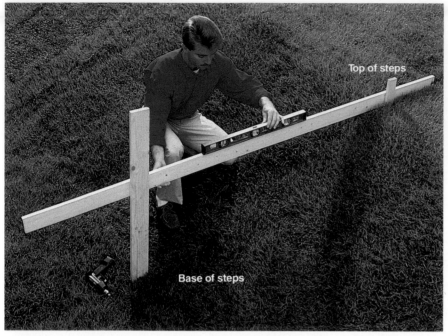

1 Drive a tall stake into the ground at the base of the stairway site. Adjust the stake so it is exactly plumb. Drive a shorter stake at the top of the site. Position a long, straight 2 × 4 against the stakes, with one end touching the ground next to the top stake. Adjust the 2 × 4 so it is level, then attach it to the stakes with screws. (For long spans, use a mason's string instead of a 2 × 4.)

2 Measure from the ground to the bottom of the 2 × 4 to find the total vertical **rise** of the stairway. Divide the rise by the actual thickness of the timbers (6" if using 5 × 6 timbers) to find the number of steps required. Round off fractions to the nearest full number.

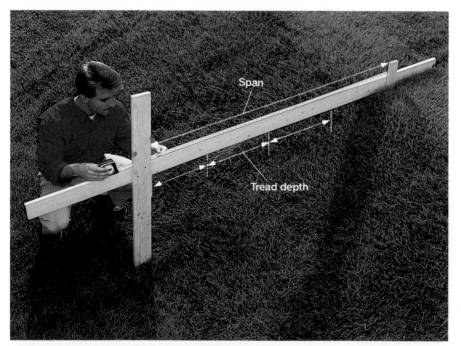

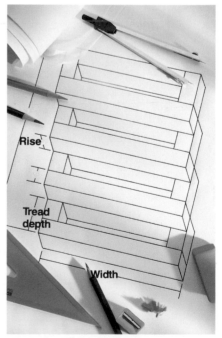

3 Measure along the 2 × 4 between the stakes to find the total horizontal **span**. Divide the span by the number of steps to find the depth of each step tread. If depth is less than 11", revise the step layout to extend the depth of the step treads.

4 Make a sketch of the step site, showing rise, tread depth, and width of each step. Remember that actual timber dimensions may vary from the nominal measurements.

1 Mark the sides of the step site with stakes and string. The stakes should be positioned at the front edge of the bottom step and the back edge of the top step.

2 Add the width of a timber (5") to the tread depth, then measure back this distance from the stakes and drive additional stakes to mark the back edge of the first step. Connect these stakes with string to mark the digging area for the first step.

3 Excavate for the first step, creating a flat bed with a very slight forward slope, no more than 1/8" from back to front. Front of excavation should be no more than 2" deep. Tamp the soil firmly.

4 For each step, use a chain saw or reciprocating saw to cut a front timber equal to the step width, a back timber 10" shorter, and two side timbers equal to the tread depth.

(continued next page)

5 Arrange the timbers to form the step frame, and end-nail them together with 12" spikes.

6 Set the timber frame in position. Use a carpenter's square to make sure the frame is square, and adjust as necessary. Drill two 1" guide holes in the front timber and the back timber, 1 ft. from the ends, using a spade bit and bit extension.

7 Anchor the steps to the ground by driving a 2$^{1}/_{2}$-ft. length of $^{3}/_{4}$" pipe through each guide hole until the pipe is flush with the timber. When pipes are driven, make sure the frame is level from side to side and has the proper forward pitch. Excavate for the next step, making sure the bottom of the excavation is even with top edge of the installed timbers.

Drive pipes here

8 Build another step frame and position it in the excavation so the front timber is directly over the rear timber on the first frame. Nail the steps together with three 12" spikes, then drill guide holes and drive two pipes through only the back timber to anchor the second frame.

9 Continue digging and installing the remaining frames until the steps reach full height. The back of the last step should be at ground level.

10 Staple plastic over the timbers to protect them from wet concrete. Cut away the plastic so it does not overhang into the frame opening.

11 Pour a 2" layer of compactible gravel subbase into each frame, and use a 2 × 4 to smooth it out.

12 Mix concrete in a wheelbarrow, adding just enough water so the concrete holds its shape when sliced with a trowel. NOTE: To save time and labor, you can have ready-mix concrete delivered to the site. Ready-mix companies will deliver concrete in amounts as small as 1/3 cubic yard (enough for three steps of the type shown here).

13 Shovel concrete into the bottom frame, flush with the top of the timbers. Work the concrete lightly with a garden rake to help remove air bubbles, but do not overwork the concrete.

(continued next page)

14 Smooth (screed) the concrete by dragging a 2 x 4 across the top of the frame. If necessary, add concrete to low areas and screed again until the surface is smooth and free of low spots.

15 While the concrete is still wet, "seed" it by scattering mixed gravel onto the surface. Sand-and-gravel suppliers and garden centers sell colorful gravel designed for seeding. For best results, select a mixture with stones no larger than 1/2" in diameter.

16 Press the seeded gravel into the surface of the concrete, using a concrete float, until the tops of the stones are flush with the surface of the concrete. Remove any concrete that spills over the edges of the frame, using a trowel.

17 Pour concrete into remaining steps, screeding and seeding each step before moving on to the next. For a neater appearance, use an edging tool (inset) to smooth the cracks between the timbers and the concrete as each step is finished.

18 When the sheen disappears from the poured concrete (4 to 6 hours after pouring), use a float to smooth out any high or low spots in each step. Be careful not to force seeded gravel too far into the concrete. Let the concrete dry overnight.

19 After concrete has dried overnight, apply a fine mist of water to the surface, then scrub it with a stiff brush to expose the seeded gravel.

VARIATION: To save time and money, skip the seeding procedure. To create a nonslip surface on smooth concrete, draw a stiff-bristled brush or broom once across the concrete while it is still wet.

20 Remove the plastic from the timbers, and cover the concrete with burlap. Allow concrete to cure for several days, spraying it occasionally with water to ensure even curing. NOTE: Concrete residue can be cleaned from timbers, using a solution of 5% muriatic acid and water.

Building a Patio

A patio can serve as the visual centerpiece of your yard and as the focus of your outdoor lifestyle. To be functional, a patio should be as large as a standard room—100 square feet or more.

Brick pavers are the most common material used for patios, but you can also build a patio with flagstone, following the same methods used for flagstone walkways (pages 74 to 81).

The most important part of a patio project is excavating and creating a flat base with the proper slope for drainage. This work is easier if you build your patio on a site that is relatively flat and level. On a hilly, uneven yard, you may be able to create flat space for a patio by building a retaining wall terrace (pages 56 to 65).

Everything You Need

Tools: tape measure, carpenter's level, shovel, line level, rake, hand tamper, tamping machine.

Materials: stakes, mason's string, compactible gravel subbase, rigid plastic edging, landscape fabric, sand, pavers, 1"-thick pipes.

Interlocking brick pavers come in many shapes and colors. Two popular paver styles include Uni-Decor™ (left) and Symmetry™ (right). Patios made with interlocking pavers may have a border row made from standard brick pavers (page opposite).

Common Paving Patterns for Standard Brick Pavers

Standard brick pavers can be arranged in several different patterns, including: (A) running bond, (B) jack-on-jack, (C) herringbone, and (D) basketweave. Jack-on-jack and basketweave patterns require fewer cut pavers along the edges. Standard pavers have spacing lugs on the sides that automatically set the joints at 1/8" width. See page 43 to estimate the number of pavers you will need for your patio.

Installation Variations for Brick Pavers

Sand-set: Pavers rest on a 1" bed of sand laid over a 4" compactible gravel subbase. Rigid plastic edging holds the sand base in place. Joints are 1/8" wide, and are packed with sand, which holds the pavers securely yet allows them to shift slightly as temperatures change.

Dry mortar: Installation is similar to sand-set patio, but joints are 3/8" wide, and are packed with a mixture of sand and mortar, soaked with water, and finished with a V-shaped mortar tool. A dry-mortar patio has a more finished masonry look than a sand-set patio, but the joints must be repaired periodically.

Wet mortar: This method often is used when pavers are installed over an old concrete patio or sidewalk (see pages 80 to 81). Joints are 1/2" wide. Wet mortar installation can also be used with flagstone. For edging on a wet-mortar patio, use rigid plastic edging or paver bricks set on end.

How to Build a Sand-set Patio with Brick Pavers

1 To find exact patio measurements and reduce the number of cut bricks needed, test-fit perpendicular rows of brick pavers on a flat surface, like a driveway. Lay two rows to reach the rough length and width of your patio, then measure the rows to find the exact size. (For a dry-mortar patio, put 3/8" spaces between pavers when test-fitting the rows.)

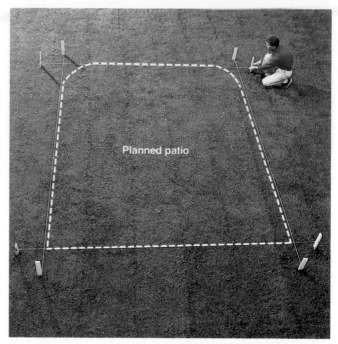

2 Use stakes and mason's string to mark out a rectangle that matches the length and width of your patio. Drive the stakes so they are at least 1 ft. outside the site of the planned patio. The intersecting strings mark the actual corners of the patio site.

3 Check the rectangle for squareness by measuring the diagonals (A-C, B-D). If the rectangle is square, the diagonals will have the same measurement. If not, adjust the stakes and strings until the diagonals are equal. The strings will serve as a reference for excavating the patio site.

4 Using a line level as a guide, adjust one of the strings until it is level. When the string is level, mark its height on the stakes at each end of the string.

5 To adjust each remaining string so it is level and even with the first string, use a carpenter's level as a guide for marking adjacent stakes, then adjust the strings to the reference marks. Use a line level to make sure all strings are level.

6 To ensure good drainage, choose one end of the patio as the low end. (For most patios, this will be the end farthest from the house.) Measure from the high end to the low end (in feet), then multiply this number by 1/8" to find the proper drop distance. Measure down from the level marks on the low-end stakes, and mark the drop distance (inset).

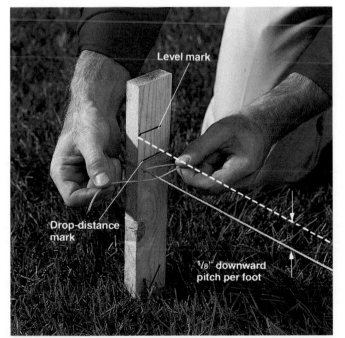

7 Lower the strings at the low-end stakes so the strings are even with the drop-distance marks. Keep all strings in place as a guide while excavating the site and installing the edging.

8 Remove all sod inside the strings and 6" beyond the edges of the planned patio. NOTE: If your patio will have rounded corners, use a garden hose or rope to outline the excavation.

(continued next page)

9 Starting at the outside edge, excavate the patio site so it is at least 5" deeper than the thickness of the pavers. For example, if your pavers are 1 3/4" thick, excavate to a depth of 6 3/4". Try to follow the slope of the side strings, and periodically use a long 2 × 4 to check the bottom of the excavation site for high and low spots.

10 Pour compactible gravel subbase over the patio site, then rake it into a smooth layer at least 4" deep. The thickness of the subbase layer may vary to compensate for unevenness in the excavation. Use a long 2 × 4 to check the surface of the subbase for high and low spots, and add or remove compactible gravel as needed.

11 Pack the subbase using a tamping machine until the surface is firm and flat. Check the slope of the subbase by measuring down from the side strings (see step 14). The space between the strings and the subbase should be equal at all points.

12 Cut strips of landscape fabric and lay them over the subbase to prevent weeds from growing up through the patio. Make sure the strips overlap by at least 6".

13 Install rigid plastic edging around the edges of the patio below the reference strings. Anchor the edging by driving galvanized spikes through the predrilled holes and into the subbase. To allow for possible adjustments, drive only enough spikes to keep the edging in place.

14 Check the slope by measuring from the string to the top of the edging at several points. The measurement should be the same at each point. If not, adjust the edging by adding or removing sub-base material under the landscape fabric until the edging follows the slope of the strings.

15 For curves and rounded patio corners, use rigid plastic edging with notches on the outside flange. It may be necessary to anchor each section of edging with spikes to hold curved edging in place.

16 Remove the reference strings, then set 1"-thick pipes or wood strips across the patio area, spaced every 6 ft., to serve as depth spacers for laying the sand base.

(continued next page)

17 Lay a 1"-thick layer of sand over the landscape fabric and smooth it out with a garden rake. Sand should just cover the tops of the depth spacers.

18 Water the sand thoroughly, and pack it lightly with a hand tamper.

19 Screed the sand to an even layer by resting a long 2 × 4 on the spacers embedded in the sand and drawing the 2 × 4 across the spacers using a sawing motion. Add extra sand to fill footprints and low areas, then water, tamp, and screed the sand again until it is smooth and firmly packed.

20 Remove the embedded spacers along the sides of the patio base, then fill the grooves with sand and pat them smooth with the hand tamper.

21 Lay the first border paver in one corner of the patio. Make sure the paver rests firmly against the rigid plastic edging.

22 Lay the next border paver so it is tight against the previous paver. Set the pavers by tapping them into the sand with a mallet. Use the depth of the first paver as a guide for setting the remaining pavers.

23 Working outward from the corner, install 2-ft.-wide sections of border pavers and interior pavers, following the desired pattern. Keep the joints between pavers very tight. Set each paver by tapping it with the mallet.

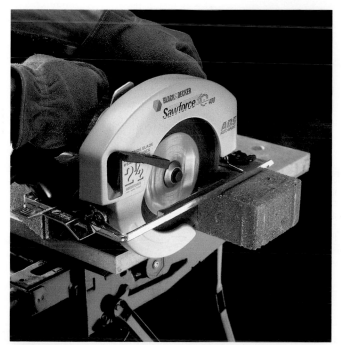

24 If your patio pattern requires that you cut pavers, use a circular saw with a diamond-tipped blade or masonry blade to saw them to size. Always wear eye protection and work gloves when cutting pavers.

25 After each section of pavers is set, use a straightedge to make sure the pavers are flat. Make adjustments by tapping high pavers deeper into the sand, or by removing low pavers and adding a thin layer of extra sand underneath them.

(continued next page)

26 Remove the remaining spacers when the installed surface gets near to them. Fill the gaps left by the spacers with loose sand, and pat the surface smooth with a hand tamper (inset).

27 Continue installing 2-ft.-wide sections of border pavers and interior pavers. As you approach the opposite side of the patio, reposition the rigid plastic edging, if necessary, so full-sized pavers will fit without cutting.

28 At rounded corners and curves, install border pavers in a fan pattern with even gaps between the pavers. Gentle curves may accommodate full-sized border pavers, but for sharper bends you may need to mark and trim wedge-shaped border pavers to make them fit.

29 Lay the remaining interior pavers. Where partial pavers are needed, hold a paver over the gap, and mark the cut with a pencil and straightedge. Cut pavers with a circular saw and masonry blade (step 24). After all pavers are installed, drive in the remaining edging spikes and pack soil behind the edging.

30 Use a long 2 × 4 to check the entire patio for flatness. Adjust uneven pavers by tapping high pavers deeper into the sand, or by removing low pavers and adding a thin layer of extra sand underneath them. After adjusting bricks, use a mason's string to check the rows for straightness.

31 Spread a 1/2" layer of sand over the patio. Use the tamping machine to compress the entire patio and pack sand into the joints.

32 Sweep up the loose sand, then soak the patio area thoroughly to settle the sand in the joints. Let the surface dry completely. If necessary, repeat step 31 until the gaps between pavers are packed tightly with sand.

Dry-mortar option: For a finished masonry look, install pavers with a 3/8" gap between bricks. Instead of sand, fill gaps with a dry mixture made from 4 parts sand and 1 part dry mortar. After spreading the dry mixture and tamping the patio, sprinkle surface with water. While mortar joints are damp, finish them with a V-shaped mortar tool (shown above). After mortar hardens, scrub pavers with water and a coarse rag.

Fences, Arbors & Trellises

Screening structures like fences, arbors, and trellises serve many functions in a landscape. They can protect privacy, improve home security, block sunlight, or diffuse strong winds. They also let you add attractive wood colors and textures to your landscape design.

Moisture poses the greatest threat to outdoor wood structures, so always choose lumber suited for exposure to water. Redwood and cedar have natural resistance to decay and insect damage, but pressure-treated pine lumber is less expensive and more durable. For a more attractive appearance, stain pressure-treated

lumber to make it resemble redwood or cedar. Use only rust-proof nails, screws, and metal connectors to assemble your wood structures.

A variety of preassembled wood panels (top photo, page opposite) is available to simplify construction of fences and other screening structures. Or, you can build your structures from standard dimension lumber. Whatever wood you choose, protect your investment by coating wood structures with a fresh coat of sealer-preservative or paint every two or three years.

Preassembled panels for landscape structures include: (A) lattice panels, (B) solid panels with lattice tops, (C) staggered board, (D) horizontal board, (E) modified picket, and (F) dog-eared board. Lattice panels, often used for trellises and arbors, are available in 2 × 8 and 4 × 8 sheets. The remaining panels, used for fences, are available in 4 × 8 and 6 × 8 sizes. Preassembled gates (inset) are available to match some panel styles. Cost of panels varies widely depending on the quality of the product.

Tips for Building Wood Screening Structures

Use metal connectors to join wood components. Galvanized metal connectors simplify installation and help strengthen the structure. Exposed metal can be painted to make it less visible.

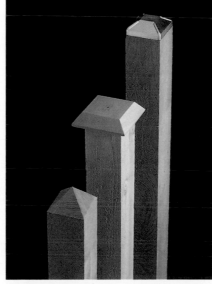

Protect the tops of posts from moisture by trimming them to a point so water will run off, or by covering them with metal or wood post caps.

Apply sealer-preservative to the end-grain of cut lumber as you build outdoor structures. The end-grain, even in pressure-treated lumber, is vulnerable to moisture and rot.

Building a Wood Fence

A fence is as much a part of the neighborhood's landscape as your own. For this reason, local Building Codes and neighborhood covenants may restrict how and where you can build a fence.

In residential areas, for example, privacy fences usually are limited to 6 ft. in height. Remember that the fence you build to give you privacy also will obstruct the view of neighbors. Avoid hard feelings by discussing your plans with neighbors before building a fence. If you are willing to compromise, you may find that neighbors will share the work and expense.

Determine the exact property boundaries before you lay out the fence lines. You may need to call the city or county surveyor to pinpoint these boundaries. To avoid disputes, position your fence at least 6" inside the property line, even if there are no setback regulations (page 37).

To ensure sturdy construction, all screening fences should have posts anchored with concrete footings. When buying posts. remember that footing depths are determined by your local

Building Code. In cold climates, local Codes may require that fence footings extend past the winter frost line.

Many homes have chain-link fences that provide security but are not very attractive. To soften the look of chain-link, plant climbing vines, shrubs, or tall perennials against the fence.

Everything You Need:

Tools: tape measure, line level, plumb bob, rented power auger, circular saw, pencil, shovel, hammer, cordless screwdriver, paint brush, pressure sprayer.

Materials: 4 × 4 fence posts, stakes, mason's string, masking tape, coarse gravel, 2 × 4 lumber, premixed concrete, fence panels or boards, galvanized fence brackets, 4d galvanized nails, 3" galvanized utility screws, preassembled gate, gate hinges and latch, post caps, galvanized casing nails, liquid sealer-preservative.

Wood Fence Variations

A panel fence is easy to build, and is well suited for yards that are flat or that have a steady, gradual slope. On a sloped lot, install the panels in a step pattern, trying to keep an even vertical drop between panels. It is difficult to cut most preassembled panels, so try to plan the layout so only full-width panels are used. See pages 104 to 107.

A low fence establishes boundaries and adds to the landscape design, but it does not block your view completely. Low fences work well for confining children or pets.

A split-rail fence is an inexpensive, easy-to-build alternative that complements rustic, informal landscapes. Building centers stock precut cedar rails and posts for split-rail fences.

A board-and-stringer fence is made with individually cut pieces of lumber. A board-and-stringer fence is a good choice if preassembled panels are unavailable, or if your yard has steep or irregular slopes. See pages 108 to 109.

How to Install Fence Posts

1 Determine the exact property lines if your fence will adjoin your neighbor's property. Plan your fence line with a setback of at least 6" from the legal property line. (Local regulations may require a larger setback.)

2 Mark the fence line with stakes and mason's string. Using a line level as a guide, adjust the string until it is level.

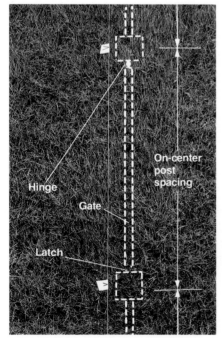

3 Use masking tape to mark the string where the gate posts will be installed. Measure gate width, including hinges and latch hardware, then add 4" to find the on-center spacing between posts.

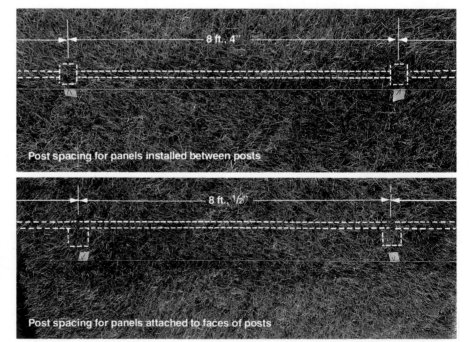

Post spacing for panels installed between posts

Post spacing for panels attached to faces of posts

4 Mark string at remaining post locations. For a panel fence, try to plan the layout so cut panels will not be needed. If your fence will use 8-ft-long panels installed between 4 × 4 posts, space the posts 8 ft., 4" apart, on-center (top). If panels will be attached to faces of posts, space the posts 8 ft., 1/2" apart, on-center (bottom). For a custom board-and-stringer fence, posts can be set closer together for greater strength.

5 Use a plumb bob to pinpoint the post locations on the ground, then mark the locations with stakes and remove the string.

6 Dig post holes with a power auger, available at rental centers. Holes should be 6" deeper than the post footing depth specified by your local Building Code. Pour a 6" layer of gravel into each hole to improve drainage.

7 Position each post in its hole. Adjust the post until it is plumb, then brace it with scrap pieces of 2 × 4 driven into the ground and screwed to the sides of the post.

8 When all posts are in position, use the mason's string to make sure the fence line is straight. Adjust the posts, if necessary, until the fence line is straight and the posts are plumb.

9 Fill each post hole with premixed concrete. Overfill the holes slightly. Check posts to make sure they are plumb, then shape the concrete around the bottom of each post to form a rounded crown that will shed water (inset). Let concrete cure for 48 hours before continuing with fence construction.

1 After posts are installed (pages 104 to 105), test-fit the panels and gates to make sure they fit between the posts. If necessary, trim the edges of the panels slightly to improve the fit (inset).

2 Mark the position of fence panels on the sides of the posts. Make sure the bottom of the panels will be at least 2" above ground level. On level sites, use a line level to ensure that the outlines are at the same level. On a sloped site where panels will be installed step-fashion, try to maintain a uniform vertical drop with each panel.

3 Attach three evenly spaced fence brackets inside each drawn outline on the sides of the posts, using 4d galvanized nails. The bottom bracket should be aligned against the bottom of the outline (inset). On the top two brackets, bend the bottom flange flat against the post. See VARIATION (next page) if panels will be attached to the front faces of the posts.

4 Slide the fence panels into the brackets from above until they rest on the bottom flanges of the lowest brackets. Attach the panels from each side by driving 4d galvanized nails through the holes in the brackets (inset). NOTE: To provide easy access for delivering furniture or other large materials through your yard, attach one fence panel with screws so it can be removed easily.

VARIATION: To attach panels to the front faces of posts, position each panel so it is level, then anchor it by driving galvanized utility screws through panel frames and into the posts. Space the screws 18" apart.

5 Attach three evenly spaced hinges to the gate frame, using galvanized screws. Follow the hardware manufacturer's directions, making sure the hinge pins are straight and parallel with the edge of the gate.

6 Position the gate between the gate posts so the hinge pins rest against one post. Set the gate on wood blocks, then attach the hinges to the post with galvanized screws.

7 Attach the latch hardware to the other gate post and to the gate, using galvanized screws. Open and close the gate to make sure the latch works correctly.

8 Measure and trim the tops of the posts to a uniform height, using a reciprocating saw or hand-saw. (If you are not using post caps, cut the posts to a point to help them shed water.)

9 Cover flat post tops with decorative wood or metal caps, and attach them with galvanized casing nails. Coat the fence with sealer-preservative or paint.

How to Build a Fence Using Boards & Stringers

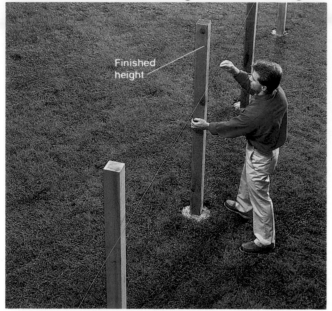

1 Install fence posts (pages 104 to 105). Mark cutoff lines on the end posts, 1 ft. below the planned height of the finished fence, then attach a chalk line to the height marks on the end posts, and snap a cutoff line across the posts. (Board-and-stringer fences usually are constructed so the vertical boards extend above the posts.)

2 Trim off the posts along the marked cutoff lines, using a reciprocating saw or handsaw. Brush sealer-preservative onto the cut ends of the posts.

3 Cut 2 × 4 top stringers and coat the ends with sealer-preservative. Center the end joints over the posts, then attach the stringers to the posts with galvanized screws or nails.

4 Mark lines on each post to serve as references for installing additional stringers. Space the marks at 2-ft. intervals.

5 At each stringer reference mark, use galvanized nails to attach a 2" fence bracket to the sides of the posts. Brackets should be flush with the front face of the posts.

6 Position a 2 × 4 stringer between each pair of fence brackets. Hold or tack the stringer against the posts, then mark it for cutting by marking back side along the edges of posts. (If yard is sloped, stringers will be cut at angles.) Cut stringers 1/4" shorter than measurement so stringer will slide into brackets easily.

7 Slide the stringers into the fence brackets and attach them with galvanized nails. If stringers are cut at an angle because of the ground slope, bend the bottom flanges on the fence brackets to match this angle before installing the stringers.

8 Install vertical boards, beginning at an end post. To find board length, measure from the ground to the top edge of the top stringer, then add 10". Cut board to length, then use galvanized screws to attach it to post or rails. Boards should be plumb, and should extend 1 ft. above the top stringer, leaving a 2" gap at the bottom

9 Measure and cut the remaining fence boards, and attach them to the stringers with galvanized screws. Leave a gap of at least 1/8" between boards (a piece of scrap wood works well as a spacing guide). Each board should extend exactly 1 ft. above the top stringer, and should have a 2" gap at the bottom. At the corners and ends of the fence, you may need to rip-cut fence boards to make them fit.

10 Attach a prebuilt gate as shown on page 107. Finish the fence by coating it with sealer-preservative or paint.

Building Arbors & Trellises

Overhead arbors and vertical trellises provide airy, attractive ceilings and walls for outdoor living spaces. They can turn an exposed patio or deck into an intimate, sheltered living area.

Standing alone, a trellis or arbor structure serves as a distinctive focal point for your landscape. Simple trellises can improve the look of a plain surface, like a garage wall, or can effectively disguise a utility area such as a trash collection space or a compost container.

Everything You Need:

Tools: tape measure, plumb bob, hammer, rented power auger, shovel, circular saw, miter saw, paint brush, T-bevel, pencil, drill and bits, ratchet wrench, cordless screwdriver, pressure sprayer.

Materials: stakes, mason's string, gravel, 4 × 4 posts, coarse gravel, premixed concrete, lumber (2 × 6s, 2 × 4s, 2 × 2s), 3" galvanized lag screws with washers, rafter ties, 3" galvanized utility screws, lattice panels and molding (as needed), 1" galvanized wire brads, sealer-preservative.

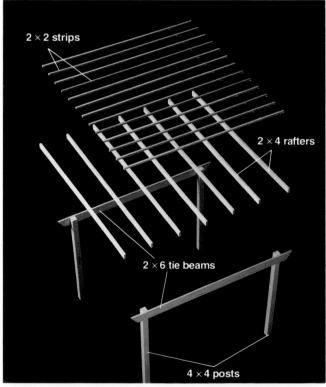

2 × 2 strips

2 × 4 rafters

2 × 6 tie beams

4 × 4 posts

Arbor structure is a simple arrangement of framing members joined to form a geometric pattern overhead. Four 4 × 4 posts support a pair of 2 × 6 tie beams, which in turn support 2 × 4 rafters. The "roof" pattern can be made with strips of 2 × 2, prebuilt grid panels, or lattice panels.

Options for Arbors & Trellises

Parallel ropes or wires make a simple, inexpensive trellis that is ideal for training annual flowering vines, like morning glories. A simple trellis can improve the look of a plain wall.

Lattice panels are easy to install, and work well to provide privacy or to block sun. Lattice panels will support lightweight climbing vines, like some types of ivy, but are not well suited for heavier vines.

Grid panels provide an airy, open surface for trellises and arbors. Grid panels work well for holding heavy climbing plants, like clematis or climbing roses.

Strips of 2 × 2 make sturdy arbors and trellises. This construction will support large hanging baskets of flowers, or heavy climbing vines, like wild grape.

How to Build an Overhead Arbor

1 Install 4 × 4 posts as directed on pages 104 to 105. Concrete footings for arbors should be at least 3 ft. deep. For arbors larger than 10 ft. × 10 ft., use 6 × 6 posts at the corners.

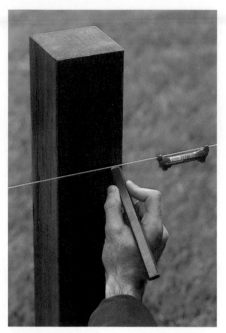

2 Mark one post at the desired height of the arbor. Mark the remaining posts at the same height, using a line level as a guide.

3 Measure and cut two 2 × 6s to use as tie beams. If you want the tie beams to extend past the posts, cut the bottom corners of the 2 × 6s at an angle.

4 Position a tie beam against one pair of posts, flush with the marked lines on the posts, then attach the beam to each post with two countersunk 3" lag screws with washers. Attach the second tie beam to the other pair of posts.

5 Mark the top of each tie beam at 2-ft. intervals. These marks will serve as a reference for installing rafters.

6 Measure and cut 2 × 4 rafters. If the rafters will extend past the tie beams, cut the bottom corners of the rafters at an angle.

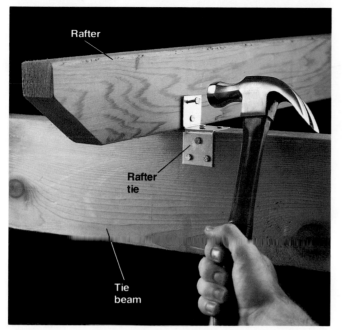

Rafter

Rafter
tie

Tie
beam

7 Position the rafters over the tie beams and align them with the reference marks. Attach the rafters to the tie beams with rafter ties and galvanized nails. Use a reciprocating saw or handsaw to cut off any posts that extend above the rafters, and coat the cut ends with sealer-preservative.

8 Finish the arbor by attaching 2 × 2 strips across the tops of the rafters, using galvanized screws. Space the strips evenly, no more than 18" apart. For denser shade, finish the arbor with lattice panels (below) instead of 2 × 2s.

How to Build a Trellis Using Lattice Panels

1 Build lattice panels by cutting sheets of lattice to size and framing them with miter-cut pieces of lattice molding. Attach the molding to the lattice with 1" galvanized wire brads.

2 Install posts (pages 104 to 105) and trim them to the desired height. Mark the posts to show where lattice panels will fit, and install three fence brackets (inset) on the sides of the posts (steps 2 to 3, page 106).

3 Slide the framed lattice panels into the brackets from above until the panels rest on the bottom flanges of the lowest brackets. Attach with galvanized nails. Apply sealer-preservative or stain to the entire structure.

113

Building Garden Ponds

Garden ponds provide a focal point and create a feeling of serenity in any yard. Ponds also expand your planting options and attract new, unusual species of wildlife.

Modern materials have simplified pond-building and made ponds more affordable. Expensive pumps and filtration systems usually are not necessary in small ponds, although they do enable the pond to support more plants and fish.

Artificial garden ponds require pond liners, which are available in two basic types: liner shells and flexible liners. Fiberglass liner shells are easy to install—simply dig a hole and set them in the ground. They are inexpensive and available in many shapes and sizes, but they may crack in very cold weather.

Most garden ponds are built with soft, flexible liners that conform to any shape and size. Some flexible liners are made from polyvinyl chloride (PVC) fabric. PVC liners are economical, but they can become brittle in just a few years.

Better-quality flexible pond liners are made of rubber. Rubber liners are more costly, but also more durable than PVC liners or fiberglass shells.

Everything You Need:

Tools: hose, garden spade, carpenter's level, hand spade or trowel.

Materials: pond liner, sand, mortar mix, flagstone coping stones, long 2 × 4.

Sizing Chart for Flexible Liners		
Liner Size	Maximum Pond Size	
	18" deep	24" deep
8 × 10	4 × 6	3 × 5
10 × 10	6 × 6	5 × 5
10 × 15	6 × 11	5 × 10
15 × 15	11 × 11	10 × 10

Flexible pond liners (above) adapt to nearly any shape or size you want. A shallow shelf holds potted plants. **Fiberglass liner shells** (below) come in many sizes and shapes. Simply set them in the ground and they are ready to stock with fish and aquatic plants.

Photo by Susan Roth

Select a level site for your garden pond. Sloping ground requires a lot of digging and does not provide a natural setting for the pond. Do not build a pond directly under a tree, since fallen leaves contaminate water and root systems make digging difficult. Ponds should not receive too much direct sunshine, however, so choose a site that is in the shadow of a tree or another landscape structure for at least half the day.

Replenish water supply regularly, especially during hot, dry weather. Ponds stocked only with hardy aquatic plants may be replenished with tap water from a garden hose. If the pond is stocked with fish, let water sit for at least three days so chlorine can evaporate before the water is added to the pond.

Collect rainwater in a barrel to replenish ponds that are stocked with fish or very delicate plants. Rainwater is preferable to city water, which contains chemical additives, like chlorine.

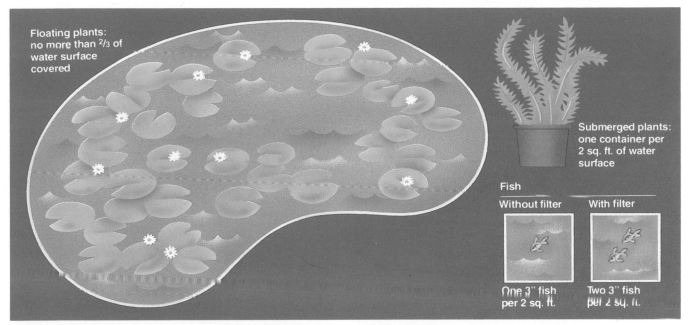

Floating plants: no more than 2/3 of water surface covered

Submerged plants: one container per 2 sq. ft. of water surface

Fish

Without filter	With filter
One 3" fish per 2 sq. ft.	Two 3" fish per 2 sq. ft.

Keep a balance of plants and fish in your pond. Floating plants provide shade for fish and help inhibit algae, but should cover no more than 2/3 of the pond surface. Every pond should have at least one container of submerged plants, which provide oxygen for fish, for every two square feet of pond surface. (NOTE: aquatic plants are available at local nurseries or from mail-order suppliers. Taking aquatic plants from lakes and ponds is illegal in most areas.) Fish add interest to your pond and release carbon dioxide that can be used by plants. Stock no more than one 3" fish per two square feet of surface if your pond does not have an aeration and filtration system. After filling the pond, let water sit for at least one week before stocking it with plants and fish. Ponds with fish should be at least 24" deep.

Planter shown cutaway

Plastic planter

Aquarium gravel

Landscape fabric

Topsoil   1" holes

Build containers for aquatic plants by drilling 1" holes in plastic planters and lining them with landscape fabric. Holes allow water to circulate past the roots of the plants. Planters protect pond liners and simplify maintenance.

Use chemicals sparingly. Little maintenance other than a yearly cleaning is needed for balanced ponds. Water-quality problems, like algae buildup, can be treated with diluted chemical products sold in pet stores.

Bring plants and fish indoors if your pond freezes for more than a week or two during the winter. Cut away plant stems, then store the plants in a dry, dark location. Keep fish in an aerated aquarium during long periods of freezing weather.

How to Install a Garden Pond with a Flexible Liner

1 Select a site for the pond (see page 116) and outline the pond with a hose or heavy rope. Avoid sharp angles, corners, and symmetrical shapes. Ponds should have at least 15 square feet of surface area. Minimum depth is 18" for plants only, and 24" if fish will be added to the pond.

2 Excavate the entire pond area to a depth of about 1 ft. The sides of the pond should slope slightly toward the center. Save some of the topsoil for use with aquatic plants (page 117).

3 Excavate the center of the pond to maximum depth, plus 2" to allow for a layer of sand. Leave a 1-ft.-wide shelf inside the border to hold aquatic planters. The pond bed should be flat, with walls sloping downward from the shelf.

4 Lay a straight board across the pond, then place a carpenter's level on the board. Check all sides to make sure the edges of the pond are level. If not, adjust the surrounding ground to level by digging, filling, and packing soil.

5 Once the excavation is completed and the site is level, dig a shallow bed around the perimeter of the pond to hold the border flagstones (called coping stones).

6 Remove all stones, roots, and sharp objects from the pond bed, then smooth out the soil base. Next, spread a 2" layer of wet sand on the level areas of the pond bed. Pack the sand with a tamper, then smooth it out with a length of 2 × 4.

OPTION: When using the more inexpensive (and more fragile) PVC pond liners, line the hole with cardboard or old carpeting pieces before installing the liner. The protective layer helps prevent puncturing and stretching of the liner.

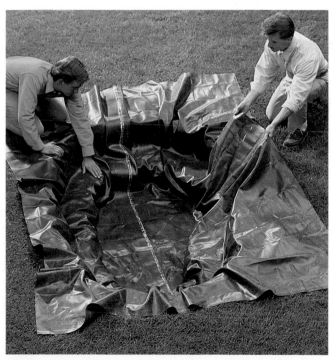

7 Place the liner into the pond bed, then fold and tuck the liner so it conforms to the shape of the hole. Smooth out the liner as much as possible, avoiding any sharp creases.

(continued next page)

8 Set a few stones on the overhang to hold the liner in place. Too many stones will cause the liner to stretch, not settle into the hole, when it is filled with water.

9 Fill the pond up to the top with water. Smooth out any large creases or wrinkles that develop as the water level rises. Remove the stones after the pond is full, and allow the liner to settle for one day.

10 Using a scissors, trim the liner so it overhangs the top of the pond by about 12" all the way around the perimeter of the pond.

11 Spread a mixture of 20 parts sand to one part dry mortar in a shallow layer on top of the liner overhang. Spray with a light mist. Set coping stones into the sand so they overhang the edge of the pond by about 2". Set one of the stones ½" lower than the rest, to serve as an overflow point for excess water.

How to Install a Garden Pond with a Liner Shell

1 Set the fiberglass liner shell in place, then use ropes to outline both the flat bottom and the outside edge of the liner on the ground. Use a level to make sure the outline is directly below the outside edge of the shell.

2 Excavate the center of the site to maximum shell depth, then excavate the sides so they slope inward to the flat bottom. Test-fit the shell repeatedly, digging and filling until the shape of the hole matches the shell.

3 Remove all stones and sharp objects, then set the shell into the hole. Check with a level to make sure the shell is level, and adjust the hole as necessary. The top of the shell should be slightly above ground level.

4 Begin slowly filling the shell with water. As the water level rises, pack wet sand into any gaps between the shell and the sides of the hole.

5 Dig a shallow bed around the perimeter of the liner to hold coping stones, if desired. Place the stones near the pond liner, but do not set them on the liner edges. Any weight on the edges of fiberglass shell could cause it to crack.

Creating a Planting Area

Use edgings around planting areas to define borders and reduce maintenance. Without edgings, lawn grass will spread into your planting area and loose-fill materials can spill out. The flexible plastic edging shown above is inexpensive and easy to install. Other edging options are shown below.

Planting areas provide a natural finishing touch to a landscape. A planting area can hold an elaborate bed of flowers, a vegetable garden, a group of ornamental trees, or a simple shrub surrounded by a bed of gravel or bark chips. Retaining wall materials (pages 56 to 65) often are used to make raised or terraced planting areas.

Make your planting areas proportionate to your yard size. Some landscape designers advise that planting areas should occupy at least 50% of the total yard space.

Unless your soil is very rich, you probably will need to add fertilizer, peat moss, or mulch to make it more suitable for planting. The type of soil builders you add depends on the quality of your soil and the kinds of plants you want to grow. To find the best soil builders, take a sample of your soil to a local garden center or a university extension service for a soil analysis.

Everything You Need:

Tools: hose, shovel, garden rake, scissors, hand spade.

Materials: see photos below.

Materials for Planting Areas

Common edging materials include: (A) standard brick pavers, (B) interlocking pavers set on edge, (C) cut-stone slabs, (D) rough stone, or (E) wood. To prevent weeds from sprouting, cover the planting area with landscape fabric (page 44) before planting, and cover the planting area with bark chips or another loose-fill material.

Natural soil builders improve the growing quality of soil without relying on hazardous chemicals. Composted manure is a mild, slow-release fertilizer ideal for all plants. Peat moss makes heavy, clay soil more workable, and it also neutralizes acidic or alkaline soil. Bone meal is high in phosphorus—an essential nutrient for fruits and vegetables.

How to Make a Planting Area

1 Outline the planting area, using a garden hose or rope. Cut away the existing lawn inside the outline to a depth of 3" to 4".

2 Dig a narrow trench around the sides of the cut-out area, and install the edging material so the top of the edging is just above ground level. Join the ends of flexible plastic edging with a plastic connector. Pack soil around the edging to hold it in place.

3 Spread any necessary soil builders over the planting area. Use a shovel to loosen soil 12" deep and work the soil builders into the ground.

4 Rake the surface smooth, and remove any rocks, sticks, and roots.

5 Lay landscape fabric over the planting area, and trim away the edges with a scissors. Cut X-shaped slits in the fabric where each plant will be located, and dig a planting hole in the soil below.

6 Transplant flowers from their containers to the planting area, then lay an even layer of loose-fill mulch over the landscape fabric and around the base of each plant. Water the area thoroughly.

Maintaining a Landscape

Protect wood structures by treating them every two or three years with sealer-preservative, stain, or exterior paint. Sealer-preservative can be applied with a pressure sprayer, but remember that these liquids are toxic. Take care not to breathe the vapors, and make sure the spray does not fall on living plants. Replace any rotted boards.

Like the other areas of your home, your finished yard requires periodic maintenance. But most do-it-yourself home landscapers soon find that yard work is more like an enjoyable hobby than a tiresome chore. Watching your landscape mature and planning new projects is all the more enjoyable when the landscape was built by your own hands.

Keep a seasonal and weekly schedule for outdoor work. In addition to weekly mowing, watering, and weeding, plan on spending some time every two or three months to inspect and repair landscape structures and tend to the seasonal needs of plants. In particular, trees and shrubs need to be pruned occasionally to stimulate good growth.

Follow the simple maintenance tips on these pages to protect your landscape and ensure your continued enjoyment.

How to Maintain a Brick Paver Patio

1 Once a year, inspect the joints between the pavers, and remove any weeds, debris, or cracked mortar.

2 Refill the joints by packing them with fine sand or dry mortar mix. Sweep the patio thoroughly.

3 Seal the entire surface with liquid masonry sealer applied with a pressure sprayer. Sealers protect the pavers from water damage and prevent weeds from sprouting.

How to Do Basic Pruning

Remove dead branches from all shrubs in the spring, using pruning shears. Also remove any branches touching the ground. Thin out the interior of the plant by cutting away branches that cross or rub together. Opening the interior of the plant to sunlight stimulates growth. Recommended pruning techniques vary depending on the species, so consult a nursery or arboretum for more detailed advice.

Shape dense hedges and shrubs using a power shears. Cutting back up to $1/3$ of the new growth helps stimulate root and branch growth. To ensure that sunlight reaches all parts of a hedge, shape it so the top is narrower than the bottom. Avoid severe pruning and shearing on needle evergreens and on flowering bushes like azaleas, rhododendrons, and dogwood.

How to Prune Tree Branches

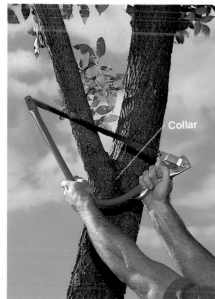

1 Make a shallow cut partway through the underside of the branch, several inches from the thickened "collar" at the end of the branch. Making the bottom cut first prevents the falling branch from stripping living bark off the tree trunk.

2 Cut through the top side of the branch until it breaks away. Be very careful if you are working on a ladder.

3 Remove the stump by cutting just outside the collar. Support the stump as you finish the cut so it does not strip away bark when it breaks free. **Do not** coat the wound with paint, tar, or sealer. These substances actually hinder the tree's ability to heal itself.

INDEX

For Product Information:

If you have difficulty finding any of the following materials featured in this book, call the manufacturers and ask for the name of the nearest sales representatives. The representatives can direct you to local retailers that stock these useful products.

Brick pavers (pages 29, 96, 99)
Uni-Group U.S.A.
  telephone: 1-407-626-4666
Pine Hall Brick
  telephone: 1-919-721-7500

**Garden pond liners, shells
  & aquatic plants (page 115)**
Lilypons Water Gardens
  telephone: 1-800-765-5459

**Interlocking concrete block
  (pages 28, 56 to 61)**
Anchor Wall Systems (Diamond Block™ and Windsor Stone™)
  telephone: 1-800-473-4452

**Landscape fabric (pages 44, 58,
  76, 94)**
Easy Garden Weedblock™)
  telephone: 1-817-753-5353

**Metal connectors (pages 45,
  72, 101)**
Kant-Sag (a division of
United Steel Products)
  telephone: 1-800-328-5934

Natural cut stone (pages 30, 64)
Buechel Stone Corporation
  telephone: 1-414-849-9361

**Perforated drain pipe
  (pages 53, 57 to 65)**
Wisconsin Tubing
  telephone: 1-800-242-8280

**Rigid plastic edging
  (pages 44, 91, 95)**
Pave Tech Inc. (Pave Edge™)
  telephone: 1-612-881-5773

Stone veneer (pages 66, 73)
Stucco Stone Products, Inc.
  telephone 1-800-225-6462

Creative Publishing international, Inc. offers a variety of how-to books.
For information write or visit our website:
  Creative Publishing international, Inc.
  Subscriber Books
  18705 Lake Drive East
  Chanhassen, MN 55317

www.creativepub.com